W9-CDC-475

Gesture, Sign, and Song

NEW CONNECTIONS
Studies in Interdisciplinarity

Shirley Paolini
General Editor

Vol. 3

PETER LANG
New York • Bern • Frankfurt am Main • Paris

Gesture, Sign, and Song

An Interdisciplinary Approach to Schumann's *Liederkreis* Opus 39

David L. Mosley

PETER LANG
New York • Bern • Frankfurt am Main • Paris

Library of Congress Cataloging-in-Publication Data

Mosley, David L.
Gesture, sign, and song : an interdisciplinary approach to Schumann's Liederkreis opus 39 / David L. Mosley.
p. cm. — (New connections, studies in interdisciplinarity ; vol. 3)
Bibliography: p.
1. Schumann, Robert, 1810-1856. Liederkreis, op. 39. I. Title. II. Series.
ML410.S4M7 1990 782.42—dc20 89-32372
ISBN 0-8204-1102-7 CIP
ISSN 0891-0073 MN

CIP-Titelaufnahme der Deutschen Bibliothek

Mosley, David L.:
Gesture, sign, and song : an interdisciplinary approach to Schumann's Liederkreis opus 39 / David L. Mosley. – New York; Bern; Frankfurt am Main; Paris: Lang, 1990.
(New Connections; Vol. 3)
ISBN 0-8204-1102-7

NE: GT

Printed by Weihert-Druck GmbH, Darmstadt, West Germany

for Karen

ACKNOWLEDGEMENTS

I wish to thank my good colleagues Randy Horst, who designed this book and assisted in its preparation, and John Roth, who read the entire manuscript in its final form. I wish to acknowledge Robert Detweiler, Douglass Seaton, and Donald Verene for their sound judgement and helpful suggestions about this project in its earlier form. I also wish to acknowledge the help of Mark Farmwald in the formatting of the Schenkerian analyses. Furthermore, Steven Paul Scher and my fellow participants in the National Endowment for the Humanities Summer Seminar "Literature and Music" were of real assistance in the formulation of many of the ideas represented herein.

Portions of this manuscript were presented to the Second International Congress on Musical Signification sponsored by the University of Helsinki and to the College Music Society at its 1989 Annual Conference. I benefited from the responses of those in attendance at these presentations. Thanks are also due to the Graduate School of Arts and Sciences of Emory University for a gift which allowed me to travel to Helsinki, Finland, and to Goshen College for a Faculty Fellowship which assisted in the completion of this project.

CONTENTS

INTRODUCTION

The phenomenon of song is an extremely complex aesthetic situation. As it existed in the nineteenth century it involved the marriage of music and poetry in an era when poets were preoccupied with the sound as well as the meaning of their verse and composers were captivated with the referential aspects of their music. Thus, an instance of song drawn from this era seems to be a logical choice for examining the many and varied relationships between word and tone, and an appropriate context to suggest a new basis for those relationships.

What is the nature of the relationship between word and tone in song and how can this relationship best be explicated? These are the central questions upon which this study is based. Any attempt to posit a theory of Lied composition presents two dangers: (1) the logocentric inclination to treat song as a literary expression, and (2) the musico-centric temptation to view song as a wholly musical expression. In other-than-musical accounts song is typically considered as little more than the incidental musical accompaniment of poetry. In musical texts it is often regarded as the thoroughly musical subsumption of poetry. However, song, and the instances of Lieder examined in the following pages, must be treated bilaterally--as an essentially hybrid expression, not unilaterally--as the domain of either poetry or music.

The theory of Lied composition outlined by Edward T. Cone in his essay "Words into Music: The Composer's Approach to the Text" falls into the logocentric category. Cone states:

> What the composer does, then, when he sets a text to music, is to choose one among all its forms...The one so chosen may have been previously obvious to every reader, or it may have been concealed to all except the composer. At any rate it might well be termed a latent form of the poem; and if you

> will forgive the word-plays, I should say that the composer's task is to make the latent form patent by presenting it through the more specific, inflexible, immediate medium of music (1957, 9).

Such a theory of Lied composition is logocentric because it treats the musical setting of a poetic text as merely another reading of the poem. Granted, Cone mentions the "specific, inflexible, and immediate" qualities of music by which the musical setting is distinguished from its progenitor. Yet, the fact remains that, for Cone, the form which music makes patent in song is a form latent in literature.

Susanne Langer's theory of Lied composition, which she explores in her *Feeling and Form,* is a part of the musico-centric category. Langer's discussion hinges upon the observation that there is not always parity between the quality of a poem and its setting. The fact that not all great songs employ equally great texts, coupled with the fact that some composers seem to prefer setting mediocre poetry, lead Langer to the conclusion that music assimilates poetry. Langer states:

> When words and music come together in song, music swallows words; not only mere words and literal sentences, but even literary word-structures, poetry. Song is not a compromise between poetry and music, though the text taken by itself may be a great poem; song is music (1953, 152).

This simply does not make good musical sense. If the musical component of a lyrical expression overshadows the literary component, why should the vocalist bother to enunciate the text at all? Why not vocalize on a single syllable and allow the music to evoke the meaning of the text?

Lawrence Kramer, in his *Poetry and Music in the Nineteenth Century and After,* posits a theory of Lied composition that transcends the logocentric and musico-centric categories by employing a psychological approach. In this work Kramer describes an agonic relation between text and music in song. Kramer states:

> A song that masters a specific text, then, does so by suggesting a new interpretation--specifically, a skeptical interpretation, one which re-writes the text in some essential way. In other words--slightly exaggerated, but only slightly--the music becomes a deconstruction of the poem (1984, 146).

Such an approach neither allows for complementary aesthetic strategies on the part of poet and composer, nor does it elucidate the correspondences between text and music which are the essence of song. Rather, Kramer's agonic theory suggests that the poetic and musical components of song are in constant combat, like soldiers in an aesthetic battle waged between poet and composer.

Steven Paul Scher, in his essay "Comparing Poetry and Music," offers still another theory of Lied composition, one based upon the principles of reader-response criticism. Scher states:

> Song compositions may be viewed as the act of the composer's assimilative reading of the original poem, as the "compenetration" of the composing reader and his text, as the cumulative process of a series of interpretive insights and operations and particularized compositional strategies called forth by the composer's reading; it is this process that I call "composed reading" (1986, 156).

In a sense, Scher's theory is something of a combination of Cone's latent form made patent and Langer's assimilation, yet it carefully avoids the myopia of each. The composer-reader of Scher's theory is similar to Cone's composer who chooses a latent reading. Likewise, Scher describes the composed reading, or musical setting, as a predominantly musical work of art which has appropriated the poet's text--an aesthetic misdemeanor compared with Langer's felonious musical assimilation.

Because of its reliance upon reader-response criticism, Scher's theory remains, if not logocentric, then at least literarily based. Such a theory may view the product, the song, as incidental to the process of reading. Yet, Scher's essay includes valuable observations on the process of Lied composition. He states:

> By placing the poetic text into a musical context, the composer-reader performs a generic transformation...In this new symbiotic construction that comprises both verbal and musical components, the words of the poem merge with and are shaped into the vocal line...(1986, 156).

Implied in this statement is the potential for equality between the verbal and musical components of Lied which arises when the poet and composer have complementary artistic strategies. Also implied in this statement is the fact that song is a conflation of poetic and musical sign systems, of poetic seme and musical gesture, to use the terminology of the study which follows.

The hybrid nature of song demands a critical stance able to treat both music and poetry with equal facility. A gestural-semiotic approach meets this requirement in that it offers the opportunity to consider both the connotative domain of the music and its influence upon the poem, as well as the denotative realm of the poem and its extension into the the music of song. In the analysis which follows the gestural component of this stance is derived from the work of the philosopher and social behaviorist George Herbert Mead. Likewise, the semiotic portion of the gestural-semiotic stance is drawn from the writings of the philosopher and logician Charles Sanders Peirce.

Although work with semiotic and music is beginning to gain an audience, and semiotic literary criticism has been employed for quite some time, this pairing of the theories of gesture and sign and their application to song is unique.[1] This approach promises to identify the shared content of poem and music in a setting, and to define the nature of the musico-poetic correspondences which are the essence of song.

[1] Wilson Coker's *Music and Meaning* (1972) is the only text to address the matter of musical signification in light of the work of Mead and Peirce, yet Coker does not examine an instance of song in his text. I am indebted to Coker for the suggestion of the pairing of gesture and sign as critical concepts, for it is his discussion of the work of Mead and Peirce that prompted my own investigation into their thought.

SIGN AND GESTURE

Logically speaking, a poem is the symbolic explication of the suppressed middle term, or enthymeme, of a metaphor. The meaning of a poem is always conventional, i.e. it is an expression based upon the triadic relation among its terms, its object or poetic content, and other related poetic expressions. Poetry consists of conventional signs, or poetic terms, placed in a specific order and exhibiting specific relations to one another which the poet deems expressive of poetic content. A poem uses actual conventional sounds in time to stand for an aesthetic idea; thus a poem is a metaphorical representation of poetic content.

A musical composition is a metaphor. In it the composer relates a tonal construction with a specific aesthetic idea. In most cases its meaning is merely possible, because most instrumental music is a unity unto itself and exhibits little referential connection to other objects or related expressions. Music consists of aural gestures placed in a specific order and exhibiting certain relations to one another which the composer deems expressive of musical content. Music makes use of certain tones in time to present or embody a possible aesthetic idea.

Song is the confluence of poetry and music, of sign and gesture, of conventional and possible meaning. It exhibits both conventional and possible connections between sound and content, and the integration of the performance of a poem with a musical structure. The coupling of sign and gesture is perhaps best suited to the analysis of song, in which a primarily linguistic, or denotative, aesthetic expression is united with a more connotative one--in which poetry is united with music. In both the title of this study and the label I have given to its critical approach, the term gesture precedes the term sign. This is because gesture typically precedes signification, or at least is the first portion of signification. Yet, in order to grasp fully the role of gesture in aesthetic expression, the domain of the sign must first be examined. Therefore, the sections which follow will deal first with semiotic and then with the theory of gesture.

Semiotic

The term semiotic literally refers to the study of signs, those things which may be used to stand for something else.[1] The subject of semiotic is typically considered to involve the denotative and connotative domains of language and their interaction. Semiotic is typically equated with the work of the Swiss linguist Ferdinand Saussure (1857-1913) who posited the critical distinction between the execution of a language, which he called *parole,* and the rules of a language, which he called *langue.* This concern with *parole* and *langue* is still the bias of European semioticians. Semiotic is less often equated with the work of Charles Sanders Peirce (1839-1914), the American logician and philosopher who outlined the first triadic model of signification and an exhaustive typology of signs. Saussure and Peirce were virtual contemporaries, each devoted a major portion of their energy to semiotic, yet neither knew of the work of the other.

Semiotic came into its own, principally as the tool of structuralism, after the turn of the century. It offered a means by which the horizontal and vertical content of structures of meaning might be analyzed. By horizontal content I refer to the successive ordering of elements and by vertical content I refer to the simultaneous ordering of elements. The horizontal content of a structure involves denotation and the vertical involves connotation. Structuralism and semiotic promised a unified approach to diverse "languages" which has not

1 Before discussing Peirce's notion of semiotic, I must offer a word about the term itself. Semiotic refers to the study of the process of signification. As Max H. Fisch points out in his essay in *Sight, Sound, and Sense,* the derivation of the term is from Greek and not Latin. Furthermore, there is no more reason for making semiotic plural, as is so common, than there is for speaking of logics or rhetorics. Therefore, I join with Fisch in his request, "I invite the reader to pronounce them (semiosis and semiotic) with me 'See-my-O-sis' and 'See-my-O-tick.' I cannot believe that Peirce ever pronounced the latter 'semmy-AHT-ick'" (Sebeok 1978, 32-33).

been realized to any great extent. Quite simply, structuralism and semiotic retained far too much of their linguistic bias and hence imposed a linguistic paradigm upon all that they approached. With the advent of post-structuralism, in which the implicit assumption that all forms of expression share certain basic structures is abandoned, semiotic has been liberated from structuralism and assumed a more active life of its own.

At its best, semiotic without structuralism has become more general and perhaps more capable of addressing non-linguistic forms of expression, and rendering new models of non-linguistic criticism. At its worst, semiotic has done little to improve upon the brand of criticism it produced in tandem with structuralism. At the same time, it has contributed to a burgeoning of jargon and a diffusion of critical purpose. A misunderstanding of the philosophical and aesthetic origins of semiotic, and their debt to the thought of Immanuel Kant, is at the heart of this floundering.[1]

Peirce's Phenomenology and Semiotic

Charles Sanders Peirce described his phenomenology, which he often called phaneroscopy, as "the description of ...all that is in any way or in any sense present to the mind, quite regardless of whether it corresponds to any real thing or not" (Buchler1955, 76). Peirce's phenomenology was greatly influenced by Kant's *Critique of Pure Reason*, which Peirce claims to have studied for two hours daily over a three-year period "until I almost knew the whole book by heart" (Buchler 1955, 2). Peirce's phenomenology shares with Kant's work an architectonic theory which holds that it is possible to derive from logic the fundamental principles basic to all human knowledge.

There are three fundamental principles, or categories, involved in Peirce's phenomenology: Firstness, Secondness, and Thirdness. Peirce stated, "My view is that there are three modes of being. I hold

[1] For an examination of the origins of semiotic in the writings of John of St. Thomas, Giambattista Vico, and Immanuel Kant, the reader is referred to Appendix One.

that we can directly observe them in the elements of whatever is at any time before the mind in any way. They are the being of positive qualitative possibility, the being of actual fact, and the being of law that will govern facts in the future" (Buchler 1955, 75). Thus, Firstness has to do with possibility, Secondness with actuality, and Thirdness with conventionality.

Peirce defines Firstness as "a mode of being which consists in its subject being positively such as it is regardless of aught else" (Buchler 1955, 76). He lists qualities such as redness, bitterness, hardness, and the "feeling of musical sound" as examples of Firstness. Matters of Firstness should be considered as phenomena without external reference. Some critics have raised the objection that Peirce's category of Firstness is rather ambiguous. Indeed, the fact that it is used to refer to monadic qualities of being is problematic; however, Peirce recognized this situation and clarified it to an extent when he stated, "The qualities of Firstness tend to merge together. They have no perfect identities. Some of them, as the colours and musical sounds, form well-understood systems" (Buchler 1955, 77).

Peirce defined Secondness as "a mode of being which consists in how an object is" (Buchler 1955, 76). Thus, Secondness necessarily demands the presence of an other. Peirce's example of Secondness is the putting of one's shoulder against a door and experiencing resistance. Peirce calls this *haeceity*, which he translates as "thisness" or "upagainstness." Secondness involves the "pairing of experience and resistance in a struggle" (Buchler 1955, 89).

Peirce defined the category of Thirdness as "a mode of being which consists in the fact that future facts of Secondness will take on a determinate general character" (Buchler 1955, 80). Peirce mentioned laws and predictions as examples of Thirdness. For Peirce, meaning is only conveyed by phenomena from the category of Thirdness (Buchler 1955, 91). Peirce concluded the section of his writings titled "The Principles of Phenomenology" with this statement:

> Here then, we have indubitably three radically different elements of consciousness, these and no more. And they are

> evidently connected with the ideas of one-two-three. Immediate feeling is the consciousness of the first, the polar sense is the consciousness of the second, and synthetical consciousness is the consciousness the third (Buchler 1955, 97).

Peirce also recognizes that although the three categories are easily enough defined and understood independently, many phenomena exist, or may exist, in more than one category.

For instance, the feeling of musical sound which Peirce tells us belongs to the category of Firstness, becomes a part of the category of Secondness when it is experienced against, or in relation to, silence or other musical sounds. Furthermore, once that musical sound is placed within the process of a composition or the continuum of musical notation it becomes conventional and thus a part of the category of Thirdness. Conversely, a logical term, which Peirce tells us is a part of the category of Thirdness because of its conventional character and the fact that it conveys meaning, also possesses aspects of Secondness and Firstness. As the term exists on a printed page for a reader, or as it is uttered to another by a speaker, it is a part of the category of Secondness which has to do with actuality and matters of fact. Furthermore, the quality of the term as it is printed with a colored ink upon paper or as it is audibilized with a particular tone of voice are qualities of the category of Firstness.

Peirce's phenomenology is extremely important to his theory of signs. The classes of signs which he posits fall under certain categories, and their ability to convey meaning is defined and delimited by those categories. Peirce defined the semiotic process in the following manner:

> A Sign, or Representamen, is something which stands to somebody for something in some respect or capacity. It addresses somebody, that is, it creates in the mind of that person an equivalent sign, or perhaps a more developed sign. That sign which it creates I call the Interpretant of the first sign. The sign stands for something, its Object (*Collected Papers* 2.228).

The notion of interpretant is the distinguishing element of Peirce's semiotic and it is of the utmost importance to the understanding of the present attempt to formulate a semiotic theory of song. The interpretant functions in both the actual and potential realms. It is an equivalent or more developed sign which enables the understanding of the representamen, and it may become a representamen in its own right, capable of determining its own triadic relationship.

The conceptual relationship between poetry and music in song is based upon the manner in which the poem, or poetic representamen, determines a musical setting, or lyrical interpretant, that exhibits the same relationship to the experience examined in the poem, or the aesthetic object, as does the poetic representamen. By lyrical interpretant I literally mean an interpretant in which word and tone are integrated in song.

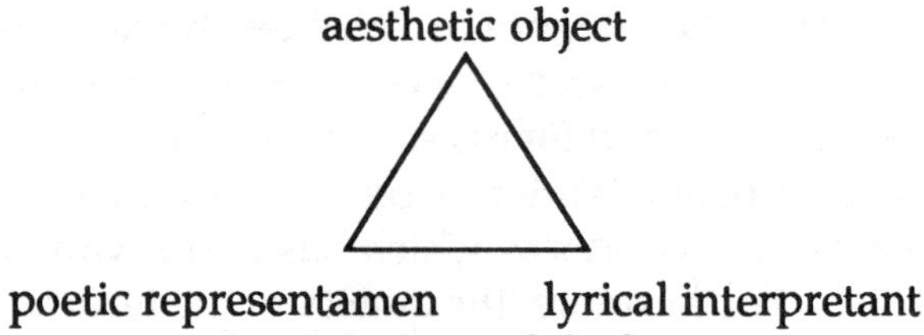

aesthetic object

poetic representamen lyrical interpretant

A semiotic model of song

The actual semiotic process in Lieder, which is the subject of this study, is more sophisticated and involves the manner in which a poetic representamen determines an interpretant which is at once an equivalent or more developed sign than the poetic representamen and able to become a musical representamen determining its own triadic relationship. I call such a sign a *melopoetic interpretant/ representamen* in recognition of its *being* a poetic interpretant and *becoming* a musical representamen. This multiple functioning of the melopoetic sign is an example of *intersemiotic transmutation* as defined by Roman Jakobson (1971, 261). It is intersemiotic because it involves the interpretation of verbal signs by means of a non-verbal sign system, i.e. the interpretation of poetry by means of the sign system of music. The transmutational quality is seen in the formal mutation which takes place in the progression from poetic representamen to lyrical interpretant, the formal change from word to tone.

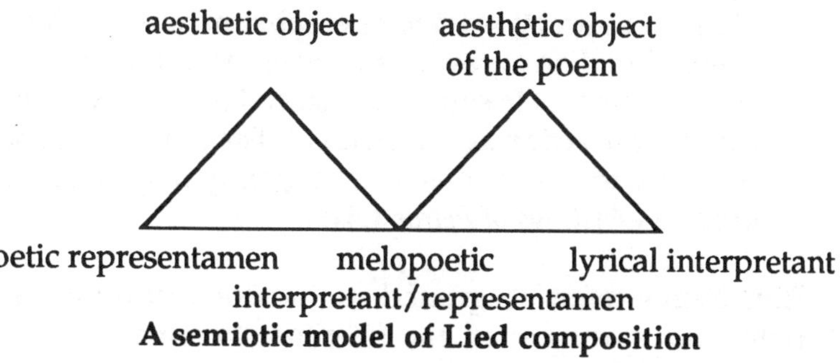

A semiotic model of Lied composition

Peirce described the relationship between any representamen and its interpretant as the ground of the semiotic process. The application of this concept to the phenomenon of song enables the identification and definition of the specific correspondences between text and music.

There are three important references to ground in Peirce's manuscripts and published writings. These come from the years 1866-1897.

> (1) Such a pure abstraction, reference to which constitutes a quality or general attribute, may be termed the ground (*Collected Papers* 1.551).
>
> (2) The sign stands for something, its object. It stands for that object not in all respects but in reference to a sort of idea, which I have sometimes called the ground of the representamen (*Collected Papers* 2.228).

And finally, in discussing the proposition "ink is black" and the relation between the immediate conception of "ink" and the more mediate conception of "black," Peirce determines that it is the quality of "blackness" that relates these two conceptions. In this regard he states:

> (3) Now this "blackness" is a pure species or abstraction, and its application is entirely hypothetical...The conception of a pure abstraction is indispensable, because we cannot comprehend an agreement between two things except as an agreement in some respect, and this respect is such a pure abstraction as "blackness." The pure abstraction, reference to which constitutes a quality may be called a ground (*Writings of Peirce* 1.515).

Thus Peirce refers to ground as: a pure abstraction, general attribute, and pure species, the reference to which constitutes a quality. Each of these descriptions show that Peirce understood the ground of semiosis to be a quality. Furthermore, as has been previously established, the triadic relationship in Lieder which unites text and music is necessarily intersemiotic. Thus the relationship between word and tone in Lieder can be described as an *intersemiotic quality*. By intersemiotic quality I mean a quality which is able to exist in both the verbal sign system of the poem and the tonal sign system of music. It must be stressed that this understanding of the relationship between word and tone in song does not account for the autonomous meaning of either the poem or the music of the setting in their entirety. Rather, it identifies and defines the specific correspondences suggested by the poem and realized in the setting.

Perhaps the most controversial aspect of Peirce's thought is the way in which, for him, signs pervade all aspects of life. He makes the statement that "we think only in signs" (1955, 115), and Kaja Silverman, in her *Subject of Semiotics*, claims:

> The point upon which Peirce here insists is that our access to and knowledge of ourselves is subject to the same semiotic restrictions as our access to and knowledge of the external world. In other words, we are cognitively available to ourselves and others only in the guise of signifiers, such as

> proper names and first-person pronouns, or visual images, and consequently are for all intents and purposes synonymous with those signifiers (1983, 18).

Yet as far as Peirce and commentators on Peirce are able to push the theory of signs and denotative signification, the limitation of his semiotic seems to lie in its inability to deal adequately with connotative signification, especially as it takes place prior to denotative signification. George Herbert Mead's theory of gesture helps to correct this limitation.

Mead and Gesture

George Herbert Mead (1863-1931) wished to understand all mental phenomena as relations between the individual and the environment. For Mead this relation includes both overt and introspective behavior, which serves to differentiate his thought from that of the more empirically minded behaviorists who followed him. He wished to show that the mind developed from society and not *vice versa*.[1] Mead's concern with prelinguistic communication is evident in the following statement in which he considers the origin of language:

> Here is a process out of which language might arise, that is, a certain attitude of one individual that calls out a response in the other, which in turn calls out a different approach and different response, and so on indefinitely. In fact, we shall see, language does arise in just such a process as that. We are too prone, however, to approach language as the philologist does, from the standpoint of the symbol that is used (1934, 14).

[1] For a discussion of the philosophical context out of which Mead's theory of gesture grows including the writings of Giambattista Vico and Ernst Cassirer the reader is referred to Appendix Two.

Three aspects of the communicative process discussed by Mead are important to this study: (1) non-significant gesture, (2) significant gesture, and (3) verbal expression.

Mead defined non-significant gesture as a preparatory attitude or movement which enables one individual to become aware of the intention of another individual. In speaking of non-significant gestures and gestural communication, Mead often used the scenario of a dog-fight as an example in which the raised fur, bared teeth, and snarling expression of the one animal are concomitant to combat but not symbolic of combat because they have only a minimal or rudimentary meaning. The non-significant gestures involved in a dog-fight carry only rudimentary meaning because they call forth an adjustive response from the second individual but they do not evoke or signify the same thing for both individuals. The non-significant gesture of Mead's dog-fight resembles the gesture of purely instrumental music in that neither carry the same significance for any two individuals, i.e. neither carry conventional meaning.

In differentiating between non-significant gestures and significant gestures, Mead states:

> Gestures become significant symbols when they implicitly arouse in the individual making them the same response which they explicitly arouse, or are supposed to arouse, in other individuals, the individuals to whom they are addressed (1934, 47).

Mead uses the term significant gesture and symbol interchangeably. One of Mead's examples of significant gesture is a boxing match in which the first individual feigns the response of being punched in order to draw a punch from the second individual. In this example the first individual calls forth in himself the same attitude he wishes to call forth from the second individual. In this situation the first individual is able to use his knowledge of the predictable response to a gesture in order to control his own conduct.

The third component of the communicative process is language itself, which Mead considered to be the union of significant gesture and idea. For Mead, vocal expression is the highest form of significant gesture because it is heard by both the speaker and the addressee. Thus, it has an advantage over physical or facial significant gestures which, though they may have a shared meaning, are not always observable by their producer.

As important as Mead's observations on gesture may be, his explanation of the process of communication breaks down when he begins to discuss significant gestures, or symbols, and their meaning.

> The response of one organism to the gesture of another in any given social act is the meaning of that gesture, and also in a sense responsible for the appearance or the coming into being of the new object--or new content of an old object--to which that gesture refers through the outcome of the given social act in which it is an early phase (1934, 78).

But the meaning of a linguistic gesture is not universally interpreted in the same way. There can be divergent responses to the same utterance, or even no response at all. The gesture does not necessarily carry universal significance to all individuals as Mead intimates in the passage above.

Mead's linguistic bias, which presents problems with types of gestures, is best understood against the background of the theories of his predecessors. Charles Darwin was extremely interested in gestures and considered them to be the conscious expression of an emotion which originated in animals and remains in humankind as an anachronism of an earlier evolutionary period. Thus Mead's linguistic bias must, in part, be an effort to offset the emotional basis of Darwin's approach. Wilhelm Wundt considered gesture as an early social act that only later becomes a symbol. Here Wundt displays something of the linguistic bias of Mead with an emphasis on symbol, yet he also exhibits a strongly behavioral bent. After discussing these two views in his *Mind, Self, and Society,* Mead made the statement, "we are prone to approach language through its symbols, not its intention which is displayed in gesture" (1934, 14).

This is indeed a bold and promising statement, but Mead does not meet its mandate. He never treats gesture as a phenomenon worthy of consideration apart from language.

In spite of these problems with Mead's understanding of symbolic gesture, his general theory of gesture accounts for the unspeakable and untranslatable aspects of human expression which lie at the heart of language and also constitute the essence of aesthetic creation. This essence is present in the manner in which the sounds of words enter into their meaning. It is present in the manner in which the materials of a visual work of art communicate a meaning which would not be present if the same work were rendered in another medium. It constitutes the entirety of most musical creation in which the experience of sound in time is without reference to any object and wholly unspeakable.

In a statement which resonates with Peirce's definition of semiotic, Mead defines the role of gesture in the communicative process: "Gestures are then that part of the act which is responsible for its influence on other forms. The gesture in some sense stands for the act as far as it affects the other form" (1934, 53). Mead's theory of gesture accounts for connotative communication and the evocation of emotion conceptually prior to signification. Peirce's semiotic is eminently applicable to poetic expression, and a combination of Peirce's semiotic and Mead's theory of gesture is equally well-suited for the analysis of the meaning of song.

The Gestural-Semiotic Method

The task of the gestural-semiotic analysis in the present study is : (1) to identify the crucial seme(s) in the poetry of song, (2) to identify the crucial gesture(s) in the music of song, and (3) to define the correspondences between seme and gesture in the song.

As mentioned earlier, the concept of gesture expands Peirce's category of Firstness. The concept of sign, on the other hand, implies symbolic expression and is thus suited for the explication of linguistic phenomena such as poetry. This is not to deny that gesture may enter into linguistic expression in the form of the actual sound of the poetic terms, nor that certain musical gestures may possess conventional meaning. Rather, the concepts of gesture and sign provide an informative and efficacious, though sometimes overlapping, approach to the complex aesthetic situation of song. The gestural and semiotic approaches are at once compatible and complementary methods. Their relation to one another and to the matter of song may be diagrammed as follows:

FIRSTNESS	SECONDNESS	THIRDNESS
MUSIC	SONG	POEM
GESTURE	→	SIGN

The combination of these two approaches in a critical study of song is revealing, simplifying, and explanatory. The concepts of gesture and sign are inherently related to musical and poetic matters, hence they are a revealing approach to these forms of expression, not a mere framework which subsumes rather than uncovers. The manner in which gesture and sign are applied to song is essentially reductive and aimed toward identifying the crucial gestures and signs of Schumann's Eichendorff songs Op. 39. Finally, this method serves to explicate the phenomenon of song in a manner coherent to the musicologist, literary critic, and performer.

The manner in which the crucial gesture of each song will be approached, identified, and explicated is based upon that aspect of music which distinguishes the musical component of song from its poetic counterpart: counterpoint and its harmonic implications. Language can exhibit moments of musicality in recitation but it can never combine voices in the manner available to music. Furthermore, the simultaneous statement of pitches is that aspect of music which distinguishes it from poetry and the one from which the gestural analysis of song must begin. The poetic component of song is likewise approached by way of its most distinctive characteristic, which is hyperbaton. Hyperbaton distinguishes verse from prose within the discursive realm of language. It is the result of the arbitrary imposition of a metrical design upon a linguistic expression, and the way to determine the influence of hyperbaton is through the analysis of poetic meter. Thus the musical gesture in song is determined in relation to the combination of sound and the poetic sign in relation to the succession of sound.

The manner in which the crucial gesture(s) of the musical component of song are identified uses the method of musical analysis posited by Heinrich Schenker at the beginning of this century (1935). His approach is reductive and based upon the recognition of normative harmonic patterns and their relation to contrapuntal motion. This method recognizes and explicates three essential levels in a musical composition and it explains the relation between those levels. Schenker identifies these levels as foreground, middleground, and background. The concept which guides the reduction of a musical composition into these three levels is prolongation; the extension of the influence of a specific pitch or pitch-configuration through a portion of a composition. Inasmuch as that pitch or pitch-configuration is prolonged, it becomes a structural element of the musical composition.

The identification of the essential poetic seme in the poetic component of song is based upon an understanding of the role of meter inspired by Roman Jakobson, who in his investigation of the relation between linguistics and poetics makes the following statement:

> From being an abstract, theoretical scheme, meter--or in more explicit terms, verse design--underlies the structure of any single line--or, in logical terminology, any single verse instance. Design and instance are correlative concepts. The verse design determines the invariant features of the verse instances and sets up the limits of the variation (1971, 161).

Accepting this primary status of meter in poetry, a five-step reductive analysis of the poetic component of song is performed making use of five types of poetic meter suggested by Northrop Frye in his essay "Melos and Lexis" (1957, xxvi). The first step of the poetic analysis consists of the standard determination of stressed syllables and the types of poetic feet. Frye calls this "prosodic" meter. The second step of the process involves the reduction of the poem to a reproduction of only those words which are stressed or contain stressed syllables. Frye calls this "accentual" meter. The third step involves the transcription of the accentual version into a prose form which represents only those salient semantic elements essential to the sense of the poem; this type of meter Frye calls "semantic." The fourth step identifies terms whose sound or meaning imitate or intimate the thrust of the poetic content; Frye calls this "mimetic" meter. Finally, the fifth step identifies terms which exhibit an oracular similarity to the poem's content; Frye calls this type of meter "soliloquizing." It should be stressed that Frye simply posits these types of meter in his essay and does little to outline a method or perform an analysis based upon them; thus the method employed in this study is original.

For each song in Schumann's Eichendorff cycle there will be: (1) a metrical analysis of the poetic component accompanied by brief remarks about the essential seme, (2) an harmonic analysis of the musical component accompanied by brief remarks about the essential gesture, and (3) an account of the intersemiotic quality which is the ground of the relationship between poetic seme and musical gesture, as poetic representamen and lyrical intepretant of poetic content.

THE MAGIC WORD AND ITS RE-PRESENTATION

Joseph von Eichendorff (1788-1857) was extremely interested in the connotative aspects of conventional poetic language. An interpretation of his poetry based upon this observation answers many questions about its means and meaning, corrects much of the misguided Eichendorff criticism to date, and explains the suggestive relation between Eichendorff's poetry and Schumann's music.

Eichendorff has long been considered a naive poet of nature whose work is filled with stock romantic images which attempt, *sui generis*, to establish an immediate relation between nature and spiritual belief. Eichendorff's poetry was extremely popular during his lifetime, yet it has received relatively little scholarly attention since his death in 1857. Recently, Eichendorff's work has become the subject of serious critical examination and regard for his poetry and prose has risen (Adorno 1958, 105-143). However important and long overdue this new regard for Eichendorff is, two distinctive aspects of his poetry are yet to be fully explicated: (1) his limited lexicon of natural images, and (2) the frequent recurrence of these images in his poetry.

The thrust of recent Eichendorff criticism is to approach his poetry as a naive metaphysics which presents a "mental landscape" populated with "natural hieroglyphics" (Seidlin 1961, 141-60). Such an approach merely clothes the earlier estimation of Eichendorff as a naive poet of nature with psychological overtones and the jargon of literary criticism. Furthermore, the matter of Eichendorff's symbols and their recurrence is recognized but is still not fully explicated.

More recent and more perceptive Eichendorff critics have recognized that the matter of symbolism and recurrence must be addressed, but, in an attempt to erect a typology of signs in Eichendorff's works, they have concerned themselves with tracing similar symbols and noting the similarity in their usage (Radner 1970, Thum

1983, 435-57). Such research is valuable for the understanding of specific poems in relation to the entire work of the poet, yet it still does not explain why Eichendorff employs a limited vocabulary and recurrent natural images.

A more rewarding approach may be to view Eichendorff's limited lexicon of natural images as analogous to the limited pitches available to a composer working within a tonal system, and that the frequent recurrence of these images is analogous to musical repetition, the principal means of organization available to the composer. Such an approach shows that Eichendorff's ultimate interest may not have been in instances of "word music" created by alliteration, assonance, or rhyme, but in the potential imitation of musical organization with linguistic constructs.

In his extremely brief and deceptively simple poem "Wünschelrute," Eichendorff states his attitude toward poetry and alludes to the role of music in his poetics:

WÜNSCHELRUTE

Schläft ein Lied in allen Dingen,
Die da träumen fort und fort,
Und die Welt hebt an zu singen,
Triffst du nur das Zauberwort.

MAGIC WAND

A song sleeps in all things,
There they dream on and on,
And the world starts to sing,
Should you strike the magic word.

In this poem Eichendorff uses the magic wand as a metaphor for the poetic term which is the vehicle for poetic conception. Just as the magic wand, or divining-rod, reveals the presence of water in the earth, the poetic image reveals the presence of song, or aesthetic potential, in objective reality.

Regard for Robert Schumann and his place in 19th century music rests upon his work both as a composer and a critic. Much has been made of Schumann's early compositions for piano in which he attempts to add a semantic aspect to his music by interpolating titles and other conventional linguistic markers in the score. Likewise, critics have attempted to show a semantic dimension in his music by claiming that it is filled with cryptic linguistic messages encoded by means of a musical cipher (Sams 1969). While such estimations make for fascinating reading, they do little to explain Schumann's music *qua* music and instead reduce it to some kind of aesthetically ornamented morse code. However misguided these characterizations may be, they do point to an important tendency in Schumann's music: he is concerned with both the expressive and the reflexive potentials of music. Likewise, Schumann's writings on music are marked by a synthesis of artistic creation and critical reflection. In these writings Schumann strives to offer a sound assessment of the music at hand and, at the same time, to present the reader with an imaginative fictional world in which the analysis takes place.

Schumann's concern with the fusion of expression and reflection can also be seen in his statements on music in general and particularly in his estimation of music's role in song in particular. In regard to music in general Schumann states:

> Musik ist die Fertigkeit, laut zu fühlen, sie ist die Geistersprache des Gefühls, welche, verborgener noch als das Gemüt, aber diese mit diesem verwoben, im Innersten wohnt. Das Gemüt muss Schmerz und Freude zuerst empfinden--wie beim Klavier die Tasten berührt werden, ehe sie klingen, dann erst teilt sich das Gefühl dem schlummernden Tonreiche mit. So ist die Musik die geisterartige Auflösung unserer Empfindung (from "Die Tonwelt" quoted in Boetticher 1941, 114-15).

> Music has the ability to express the emotions audibly; it is the

> spiritual language of emotion, which is hidden more secretly than the soul; but one interwoven with the other dwells in the innermost region. The soul must first perceive pain and joy--just as at the piano the keys must be touched before they sound; it is only then that the emotion communicates with the slumbering realm of the tones. Thus music is the spiritual expression/reflection of our sensations.

The crucial term used by Schumann in reference to music in this passage is *Auflösung*, which in Schumann's estimation constitutes the essential function of music. What has until now been overlooked in this passage, which is otherwise filled with romantic platitudes about music and its evocative powers, is the sense in which music is at once the expression of, and, a reflection upon, emotion. Such a dual meaning is contained in the term *Auflösung* which refers to the release of tension and the solution of a problem.

This expressive and reflexive function of music is alluded to in many of Schumann's statements on song. Schumann praised and practiced what he considered to be a new style of song-setting which abandoned formulaic accompaniment and did not take as its impetus the imitation of surface elements in the poem: i.e. those elements of the poem which recommend themselves to music but do little to convey the essence of the text. In a review praising this "new style" in the songs of his contemporary Robert Franz, Schumann states:

> ...er will uns das Gedicht in seiner leibhaftigen Tiefe wiedergeben (*Gesammelte Schriften* II, 348).

> ..he strives to represent an embodiment of the poem.

Thus the quality of Franz's songs which Schumann values is the manner in which they reproduce, or re-present, the meaning of the poetic conception; the way in which the song translates the poetic expression into a musical expression and presents again the poem's essence. Such a re-presentation is at once expressive and reflexive, inasmuch as it conveys the meaning of the poem translated both in and into another medium. In reference to Norbert Burgmüller's Op. 10, Schumann states:

> Das Gedicht mit seinen kleinsten Zügen im feineren musikalischen Stoffe nachzuwirken, gilt ihm das Höchste, wie es Allen gelten sollte (*Gesammelte Schriften* II, 175).
>
> He regards it--as everybody should--as the highest task to recapture the poem in its smallest detail with finer musical material.

This statement should not be read as contradicting the previous statement about the songs of Robert Franz. In each of these passages Schumann is referring to music's representative powers. His praise of Burgmüller's attention to detail is based upon the composer's thorough and empathetic understanding of the poem, not the mere imitation of surface detail. Both *nachwirken* and *wiedergeben* refer to the way in which music re-presents, or stands for, the poem in its totality. Thus, Schumann is concerned with re-presenting a poem not simply by means of imitation, but through the translation of its salient characteristics into another aesthetic system.

As I have described it, a gestural-semiotic theory of Lied composition is able to account for complementary aesthetic strategies on the part of both the poet and the composer. In the case of Eichendorff's poetics and Schumann's musical aesthetics, this theory of Lied composition is applicable in the following manner. Eichendorff's magic word functions as the poetic representamen, the sign which unlocks the aesthetic potential in all things. And the song of Eichendorff's poem, which sleeps in all things, is the lyrical interpretant of the magic word. For Eichendorff, poetry and song are analogous signs of the same object, and the presence of song is a verification that the poetic term has tapped the potential of that object. As is seen in his use of *nachwirken*, Schumann is concerned with representing a poem's meaning not simply by means of imitation, but through the translation of its essence into another aesthetic system. Furthermore, the fact that Schumann conceives of music as both expressive and reflexive is mirrored in the manner in which the melopoetic interpretant/representamen simultaneously provides an hermeneutic view of the poetic representamen and creates a new musical representamen capable of determining its own triadic relationship.

THE POETIC REPRESENTAMEN AND ITS LYRICAL INTERPRETANT

This poem is from the *Totenopfer* section of Eichendorff's collected works. Eichendorff divided his writings into eight categories and classified his poems accordingly. The poems in Schumann's *Liederkries* Op. 39 come from six of these eight divisions. The entire song cycle was composed during the spring of 1840 prior to the marriage of Schumann and Clara Weick. This poem is a dream-like contemplation of the relation between nature and altered states of being. The context of the dream, and the evolving significance of images encountered in this state, is the context which seems to have informed Schumann's selection and ordering of the poems in this cycle.

I. Prosodic

IN DER FREMDE

Aus der Heimat hinter den Blitzen rot,
Da kommen die Wolken her,
Aber Vater und Mutter sind lange tot,
Es kennt mich dort keiner mehr.

Wie bald, wie bald kommt die stille Zeit,
Da ruhe ich auch, und über mir
Rauschet die schöne Waldeinsamkeit,
Und keiner mehr kennt mich auch hier.

I. Accentual

IN DER FREMDE

Heimat hinter Blitzen rot
kommen Wolken her
Vater Mutter lange tot
kennt keiner mehr

bald, bald stille Zeit
ruhe auch, über mir
Rauschet schöne Waldeinsamkeit
keiner kennt hier

I. Semantic

IN DER FREMDE

Vater Mutter lange tot kennt keiner mehr

Rauschet schöne Waldeinsamkeit keiner kennt hier

I. Mimetic

IN DER FREMDE

die stille Zeit

I. Soliloquizing

IN DER FREMDE

Waldeinsamkeit

Eichendorff's poem examines the inexorability of time and the threatening inevitability of death in a dream-like state. It attempts to mitigate this threat through various observations and assertions. In the line "aber Vater und Mutter sind lange tot" the poem recognizes that death has existed in the past. In the line "wie bald, wie bald kommt die stille Zeit" it recognizes that death will come in the future. More than any other, the phrase "schöne Waldeinsamkeit" attempts to mitigate the threatening nature of altered states of being, including death, through its euphemistic qualities. This phrase suggests that, perhaps, death is no worse than solitude in nature.

The crucial seme of this poem is the euphemism *Waldeinsamkeit*. As a poetic representamen, this term can determine any number of interpretants. Some of these interpretants are, no doubt, likely to be other poetic terms which are similar in form or function. For instance, "Waldeinsamkeit" is similar in form to the common romantic image of "Waldfriedhof;" and the notion of a small graveyard in the forest is arguably an equivalent or more developed sign than "Waldeinsamkeit" and thus capable of serving as an interpretant. The poetic representamen may also be grasped within the sign system of language in a functional or rhetorical manner. In this case a possible interpretant for "Waldeinsamkeit" is the concept of euphemism.

LIEDERKREIS

Zwölf Gesänge von J. von Eichendorff

für eine Singstimme mit Begleitung des Pianoforte

von

Schumann's Werke. Serie 13. № 9.

ROBERT SCHUMANN.

Op. 39.

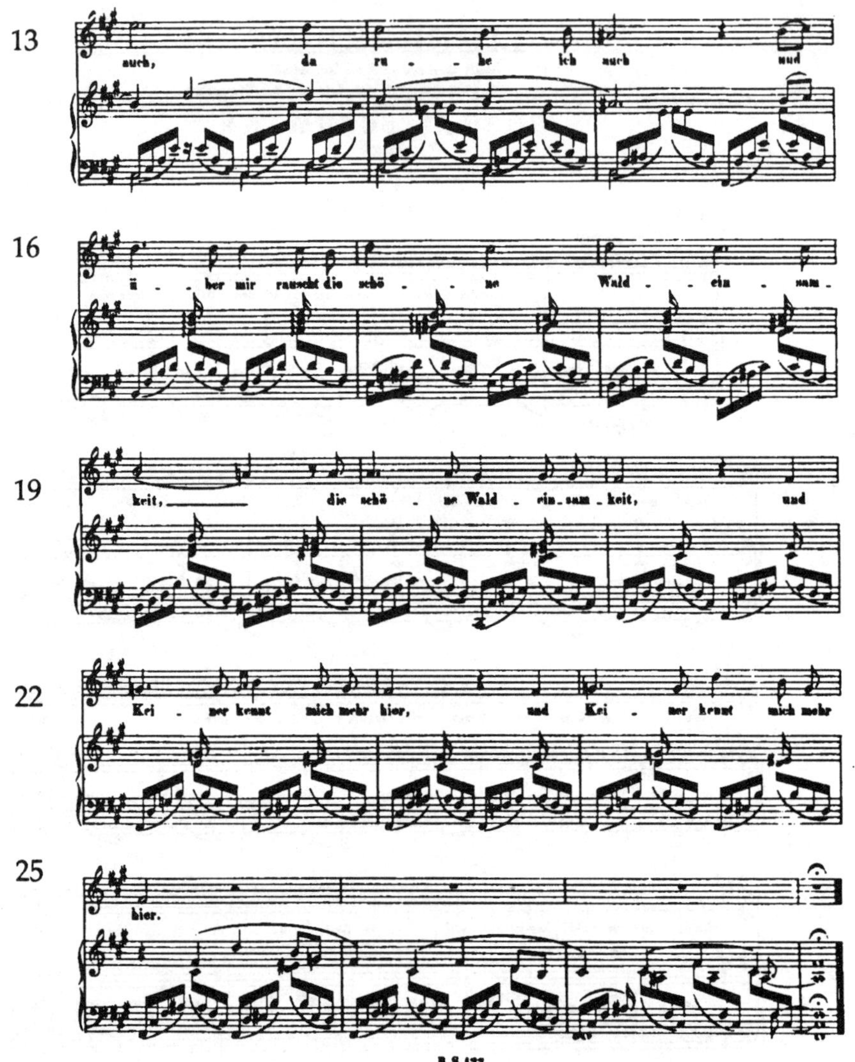
13
auch, da ru - he ich auch und
16
ü - ber mir rauscht die schö - ne Wald - ein - sam -
19
keit, die schö - ne Wald - ein - sam - keit, und
22
Kei - ner kennt mich mehr hier, und Kei - ner kennt mich mehr
25
hier.

R.S.127.

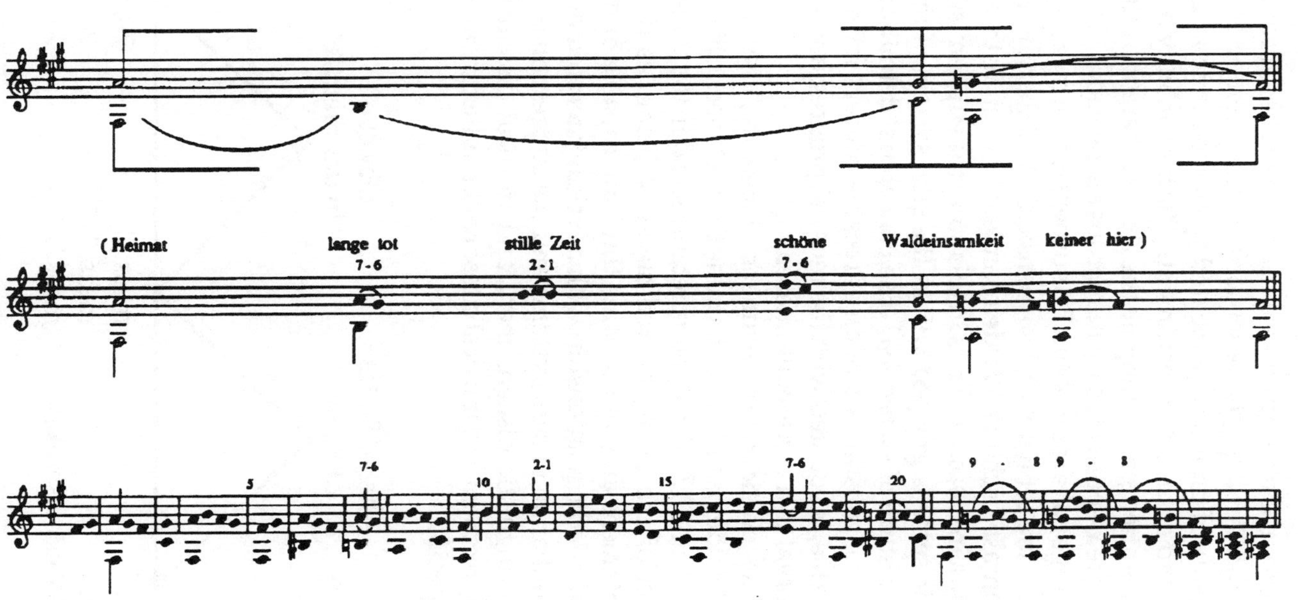
No. 1 In der Fremde
(Heimat
lange tot
7-6
stille Zeit
2-1
schöne
7-6
Waldeinsamkeit
keiner hier)
5
7-6
10
2-1
15
7-6
20
9 - 8 9 - 8

Schumann's setting re-presents the rationalizations, recognitions, and euphemistic assertions of the poem musically. The inexorability of time is re-presented by the continuous sixteenths in the left hand of the accompaniment. The inevitability of death, and the poem's attempts to mitigate the threat inherent in altered states of being, are re-presented by numerous suspensions. In meas. 7 the words "lange tot" are set with a 7-6 suspension. In meas. 11 the words "stille Zeit" are set with a 2-1 suspension. And the adjective "schön" of the phrase "schöne Waldeinsamkeit" is set with another 7-6 suspension in meas. 17. Thus in this song the euphemistic nature of the poetic seme is grasped within the sign system of music by the musical gesture of *suspension*. The conceptual definition of euphemism, as the substitution of an agreeable concept for one which is disagreeable, is equated with the musical progression from a dissonant interval to a consonant interval.

The poetic representamens "lange tot," "stille Zeit," and "schöne Waldeinsamkeit" determine the melopoetic interpretants of meas. 7, 11, and 17. These interpretants stand in the same relation to the object of the poem, altered states of being, as do the poetic representamens and, at the same time, are capable of determining their own triadic relationship with a lyrical interpretant. Of course such a conflation of sign systems and the suggestion of an analogy between linguistic disagreement and musical dissonance, or linguistic agreement and musical consonance, is historically and stylistically specific.

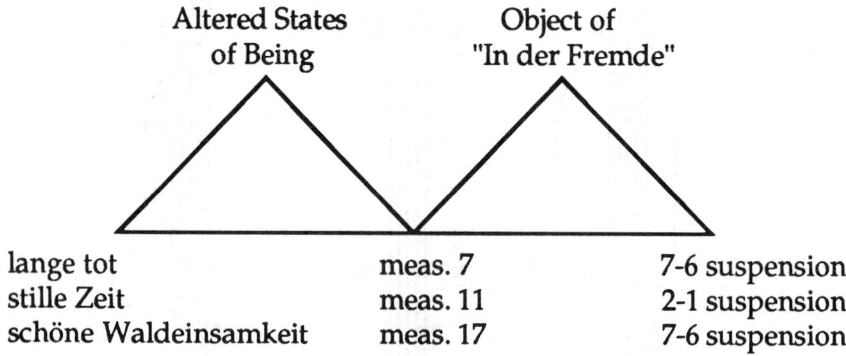

The lyrical proposition of this song involves the manner in which the poem as representamen determines a musical setting as interpretant, both of which stand in the same relation to the object of altered states of being. The ground of this relationship, the intersemiotic quality which is shared by both the poem and setting in relation to the object, is *mitigation*. Mitigation is a pure abstraction, reference to which constitutes a quality, i.e. the pure feeling of a reduction in tension. This quality is present in the euphemistic function of the poetic representamens and their relation to altered states of being, as well as in the voice-leading device of suspension and its relation to the object of "In der Fremde."

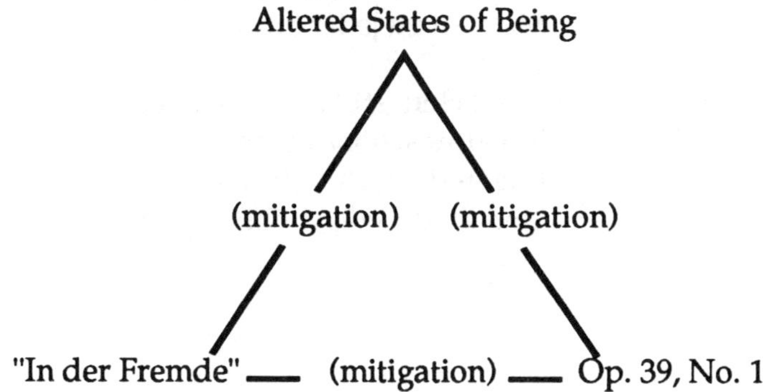

Eichendorff's "Andenken" comes from the *Sangerleben* section of his work. The poem examines the power which the memory of the beloved exerts as a poetic image. Schumann changes the title to "Intermezzo" in his setting.

II. Prosodic

ANDENKEN

Dein Bildnis wunderselig
Hab' ich im Herzensgrund,
Das sieht so frisch und fröhlich
Mich an zu jeder Stund'.

Mein Herz still in sich singet
Ein altes schönes Lied,
Das in die Luft sich schwinget
Und zu dir eilig zieht.

II. Accentual

ANDENKEN

Bildnis wunderselig
hab' Herzensgrund
sieht frisch fröhlich
jeder Stund'

Herz still singet
altes schönes Lied
das Luft schwinget
eilig zieht

II. Semantic

ANDENKEN

Bildnis hab' Herzensgrund

Herz singet Lied eilig zieht

II. Mimetic

ANDENKEN

altes schönes Lied

II. Soliloquizing

ANDENKEN

Herzensgrund
Herz singet

Eichendorff's "Andenken" presents a situation in which a poem filled with typical poetic language and unremarkable grammatical constructions conveys a powerful statement. In many ways, this situation is most typically Eichendorffian and it is this kind of expression that has has caused most critics and generations of readers to relegate Eichendorff to minor status in the world of nineteenth-century romantic poetry. Though the characteristics of formal control, economy of means, and unified composition are most frequently applied to classical expressions, they may also serve as an indispensable foil for the romantic poet.

This poem addresses the manner in which the image of the beloved in memory serves as a sign of the love relationship, and at the same time generates interpretants, or analogous signs, which take on a semiotic life of their own. The interpretant, or analogous sign, of the image of the beloved is singing. Eichendorff seems to suggest that the heart is able to transform the image of the beloved into an expression of the beloved. The transformation is from memory into song; from passive reflection into active expression. A reduction and paraphrase of this poem might read: "Your image in my heart causes my heart to sing to you." This paraphrase alludes to the point made in reference to Eichendorff's poetics as expressed in his poem "Wünschelrute" regarding the aesthetic potential in objective reality. The crucial semes of the poem are *Herzensgrund* and *Herz singet* which suggest the multiple function of memory.

Intermezzo.
Nº 2.
Langsam.
Dein Bild - niss wun - der - se - lig hab' ich im Her - zens -
5
grund, das sieht so frisch und fröh - lich mich an zu je der
9
p nach und nach schneller
Stund'. Mein Herz still in sich sin - get ein al - tes schö - nes
13
und schneller
Lied, das in die Luft sich schwin - get und zu dir ei - lig
17
ritard. Im Tempo.
zieht. Dein Bild - niss wun - der - se - lig, hab' ich im Her - zens -

21
grund; das sieht so frisch und fröh_lich mich an zu je_der, je_der
ritard.
ritard.
p
25
Stund'.
ritard.

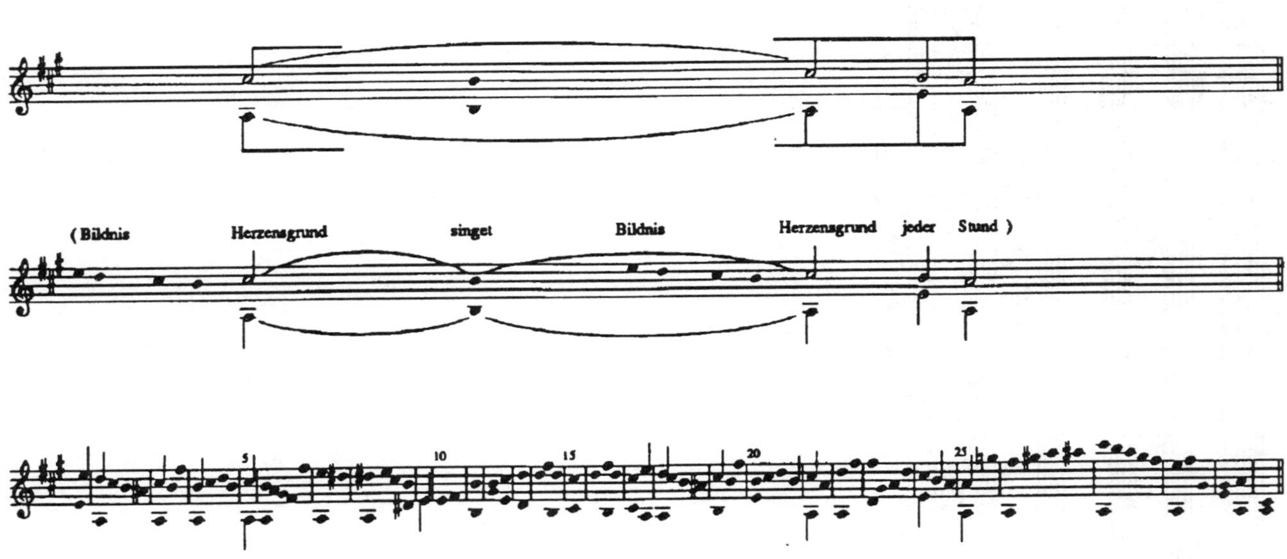
No. 2 Intermezzo
(Bildnis Herzensgrund singet Bildnis Herzensgrund jeder Stund)
5
10
15
20
25

Given Schumann's aesthetics of music in which musical expression is both expressive and reflexive, it is easy to understand his attraction to this poem. In his setting of "Andenken" Schumann changes the title to "Intermezzo" and repeats the first strophe after the second strophe. Although this change in title may seem a rather innocuous attempt to place the poem in more of a musical context in the *Liederkreis*, it is an important clue for understanding this setting's structural role in the cycle as a whole. Schumann's use of this term may suggest that this song is to serve a connecting or bridging function between "In der Fremde" and "Waldesgespräch" to follow.

The crucial gesture in Schumann's setting of "Andenken" is the *pitch configuration* in which the pitch B serves to connect the two major thirds as a lower neighbor to the C#, an upper neighbor to the A, and a passing tone between C# and A. This multiple function of the pitch B clearly imitates the function of the term *Herz* in Eichendorff's poem. Furthermore, the fact that statements of *Herzensgrund* in meas. 5 and 21 involve a C# in the voice over a prolongation of A in the left hand of the accompaniment, and the statement of *Herz singet* involves a B in the voice over a B in the left hand of the accompaniment, articulates the harmonic infrastructure.

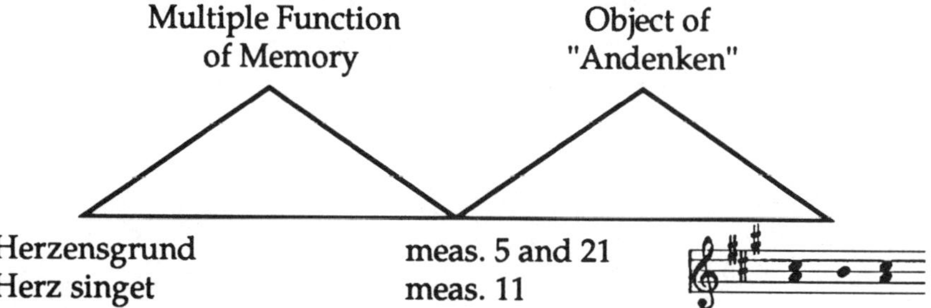

The ground of the intersemiotic relationship between the poem and its setting in Op. 39, No. 2 is *equivocation*. In a linguistic sense, equivocation is the use of a term with a double meaning. Eichendorff uses *Herz* as a metaphor to signify both reflection and expression, it is both the repository of memory and the origin for the expression of love. Likewise, Schumann's setting makes use of an harmonic construction turning upon a single pitch which functions as a lower neighbor, upper neighbor, and passing tone.

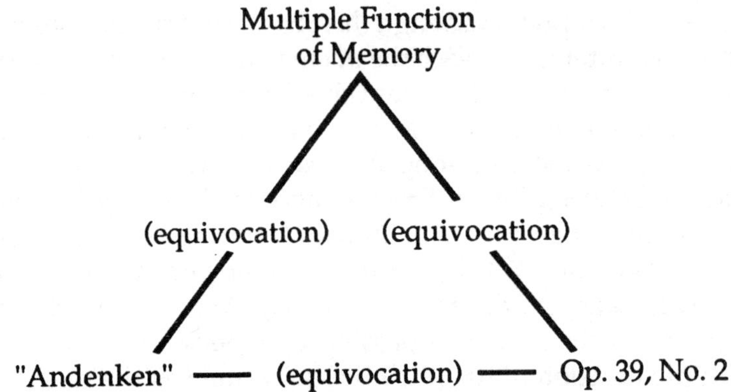

Eichendorff's "Waldesgespräch" comes from the *Romanzen* section of his collected works. It presents a dramatic dialogue between a young male traveler and the sorceress Lorelei. Schumann changes the first line to "Es ist schon spät, es ist schon kalt."

III. Prosodic

WALDESGESPRÄCH

"Es ist schon spät, es wird schon kalt,
Was reitst du einsam durch den Wald?
Der Wald ist lang, du bist allein,
Du schöne Braut! Ich führ' dich heim!"

"Gross ist der Männer Trug und List,
Vor Schmerz mein Herz gebrochen ist,
Wohl irrt das Waldhorn her und hin,
O flieh! du weisst nicht, wer ich bin."

"So reich geschmückt ist Ross und Weib,
So wunderschön der junge Leib,
Jetzt kenn' ich dich--Gott steh' mir bei!
Du bist die Hexe Lorelei."

"Du kennst mich wohl--von hohem Stein
Schaut still mein Schloss tief in den Rhein.
Es ist schon spät, es wird schon kalt,
Kommst nimmermehr aus diesem Wald!"

III. Accentual

WALDESGESPRÄCH

ist spät wird kalt
reitst einsam durch Wald
Wald lang bist allein
schöne Braut führ' heim

gross Männer Trug List
Schmerz Herz gebrochen ist
irrt Waldhorn her hin
flieh weisst (nicht) wer bin

reich geschmückt Ross Weib
wunderschön junge Leib
kenn' dich Gott bei
bist Hexe Lorelei

kennst wohl hohem Stein
still Schloss tief Rhein
ist spät wird kalt
nimmermehr aus Wald

III. Semantic

WALDESGESPRÄCH

reitst einsam schöne Braut?

flieh weisst (nicht) wer

kenn' dich--Gott (steh' mir) bei!

nimmermehr aus Wald!

III. Mimetic

WALDESGESPRÄCH

allein/heim
Stein/Rhein

III. Soliloquizing

WALDESGESPRÄCH

Lorelei!

This poem is not so much about the supernatural power of a beautiful sorceress, as it is about the irrational aspects of the attraction to beauty. "Waldesgespräch" presents a situation in which beauty and attraction become fearful matters. A part of this richer treatment of one of the favorite romantic topics is the information Eichendorff gives the reader about the Lorelei, i.e. she has been hurt in love and tries to warn the young man about the dangers of involvement with her. This information also enriches the characterization of the young man who continues to pursue conversation with the Lorelei even after her warning.

Eichendorff symbolizes and signifies this irrational situation by means of rhyme. In a very real way, a rhyme is the creation of a relation or attraction between two terms which do not ordinarily exhibit such a relation or attraction. A rhyme is built upon sound and not upon sense, thus it too can be termed irrational.

The poem's rhyme scheme, like its prosodic scansion, is almost wholly regular. The one exception is the pseudo-rhyme "allein/ heim." This rhyme occurs at the moment in the poem when the young man reiterates the fact that the woman is traveling alone and offers to accompany her home. This rhyme brings together semantic issues which are opposed in nature; "allein" suggests loneliness and danger, while "heim" suggests companionship and safety. This rhyme is related to two other important rhymes in the poem by virtue of its assonant quality: "bei/Lorelei" and "Stein/Rhein." The first of these related rhymes brings together the notions of Christianity (Gott steh' mir bei!) and witchcraft (Lorelei), and the second the notions of height and and depth.

The rhyme of "Stein/Rhein" places the notions of height and depth in the context of a cliff overlooking a river which is a traditional setting of great beauty and typically functions as such within Eichendorff's symbology; yet there is an attraction to such a scene which is irrational and dangerous as well, as anyone who has ever stood on a precipice and looked out over a vast and beautiful expanse knows. The attraction seems to be grounded in the beauty of the scene, the void between the observer and the beauty, and the human desire to appropriate beauty. The same situation exists between the young man and the Lorelei. She exhibits beauty, she is distant from him, and he desires union with her. Yet as the union with the beauty that lies beyond or beneath a great precipice involves great danger, so does union with the crucial seme of the poem--the *Lorelei*.

Nº 3.
Waldesgespräch.
Ziemlich rasch.
mf
Es ist schon
spät, es ist schon kalt, was reit'st du ein - sam durch den
Wald? Der Wald ist lang, du bist al - lein, du schö - ne Braut, ich führ' dich
R.S.127.

15
heim! Gross ist der Män - ner Trug und List, vor
21
Schmerz mein Herz ge - bro - chen ist, wohl irrt das Wald - horn
27
her und hin, o flieh'! o flieh'! du weisst nicht, wer ich bin.
33
So reich ge - schmückt ist Ross und Weib, so wun - der - schön, so
38
ritard.
Im Tempo.
wun - der - schön der jun - ge Leib; jetzt kenn' ich dich, Gott steh' mir bei, du
ritard.
Im Tempo.

43
ritard.
Im Tempo
bist die Hexe Lo - re - ley!
Du kennst mich wohl, du
49
kennst mich wohl, von hohem Stein schaut still mein Schloss tief in den
54
Rhein; es ist schon spät, es ist schon kalt, kommst
60
ritard.
nim-mermehr aus die-sem Wald, nim - mer - mehr, nim - mer - mehr aus die - sem Wald.
65
ritard.
R.S.137.

No. 3 Waldesgespräch

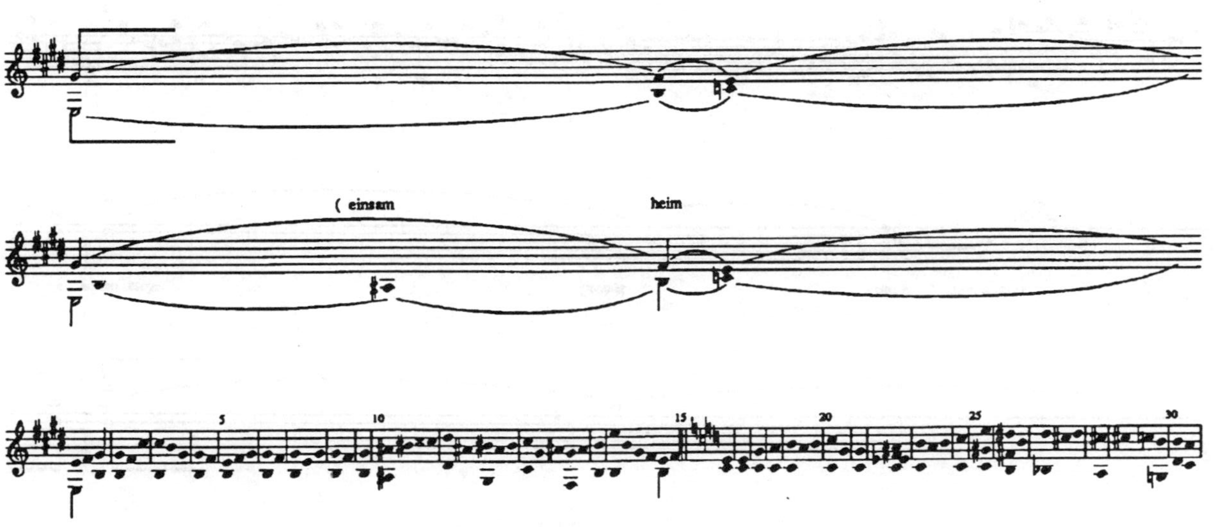

No. 3 continued

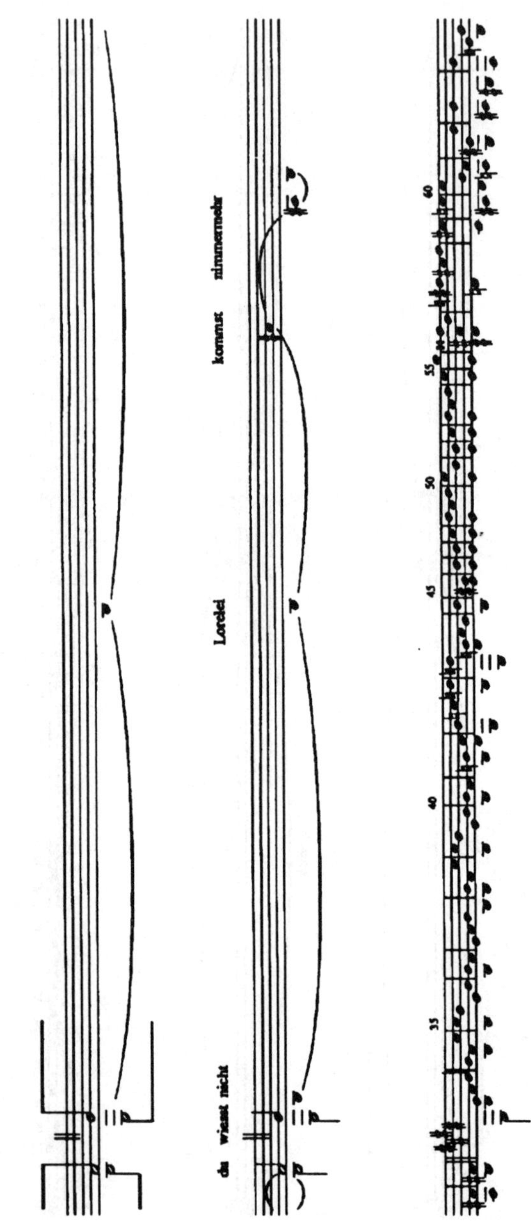

No. 3 continued

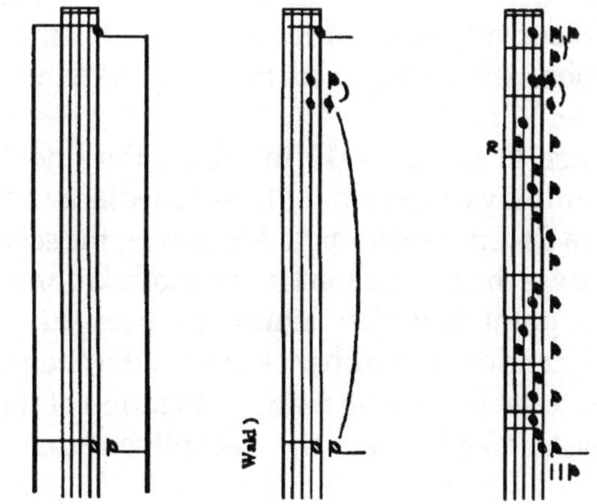

The process of setting a poem based upon dialogue to music points out many important characteristics of the acoustic component of song. First of all, a song is able to embody and depict characters in a more literal way than a poem. Eichendorff's text signals the shift in speakers by means of quotation marks and alternating strophes. While these are certainly adequate markers, music is able to do much more through register, rhythm, and harmony. Even though a single voice will perform the song, the signals for the shift in speakers are clearer, more realistic, and of longer duration in the setting than in the poem.

Schumann chooses to use harmony and register to differentiate the young man and the Lorelei in his setting of "Waldesgespräch." In general, the first and third strophes are set with a lower and thus more masculine melodic line, while the second and fourth strophes are set with a higher and more feminine line. This distinction is emphasized in meas. 36 which asks the singer for a low B and in meas. 55 which demands a high G#. In each case Schumann wrote alternate pitches because these extremes of register are difficult for even the most well-trained voice.

Since the signal of register might well be modified in performance, the matter of harmony is thus even more important in regard to alternating voices. Schumann sets the two strophes involving statements by the young man in E major. He sets the first of the Lorelei's strophes in C major and the second in E major with a great deal of chromaticism and secondary function. The specific harmonic motion and a specific cadence within this motion, however, does much more than simply distinguish the young man's voice from that of the Lorelei.

The cadence in meas. 14-15 in which the line "ich führ' dich heim!" is set employs a dominant to submediant movement in the bass, creating a deceptive cadence. Moreover, the second half of this cadential figure is the pivot chord in the modulation from E major to C major. The point at which Schumann uses this cadence corresponds to Eichendorff's assonance on "allein/heim." This same device is used to set the young man's realization of the Lorelei's true identity in meas. 43-44. Here the deceptive cadence moves from dominant to mediant, and the second half of the cadence is the pivot chord in the modulation to E major. The conventional understanding of the deceptive cadence, as implied in its name, is that of an unexpected resolution. The crucial musical gesture of Schumann's setting is the *deceptive cadence*.

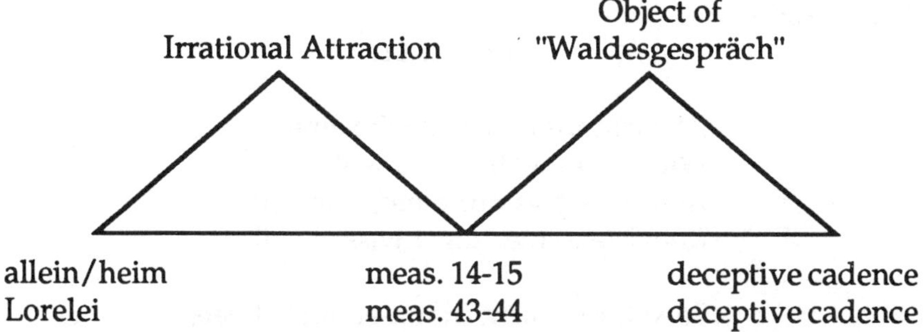

The ground of the intersemiotic relationship between Eichendorff's poem and Schumann's setting is *deception*. Deception is the mode of discourse between the young man and the Lorelei. Furthermore, deception is present in the poem in the manner in which unrelated and even opposing terms are joined together by assonance. Likewise, Schumann's setting makes use of a surprising and bewildering aural experience, that of a deceptive cadence, as a musical interpretant for the poem's deceptive discourse.

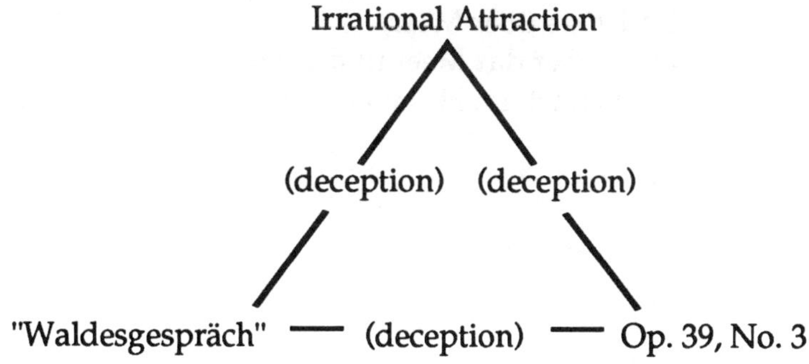

Eichendorff's "Die Stille" comes from the *Frühling und Liebe* section of his collected works. In the poem, the female narrator savors her secret love and contemplates sharing it with her beloved. Schumann omits the third strophe and instead repeats the first as a conclusion. He also changes the last word of line one to "sollt'."

IV. Prosodic

DIE STILLE

Es weiss und rät es doch keiner,
Wie mir so wohl ist, so wohl!
Ach, wüsst' es nur einer, nur einer,
Kein Mensch es sonst wissen soll!

So still ist's nicht draussen im Schnee,
So stumm und verschweigen sind
Die Sterne nicht in der Höh',
Als meine Gedanken sind.

Ich wünscht', es wäre schon Morgen,
Da fliegen zwei Lerchen auf,
Die überfliegen einander,
Mein Herze folgt ihrem Lauf.

Ich wünscht', ich wäre ein Vöglein
Und zöge über Meer,
Wohl über das Meer und weiter,
Bis dass ich im Himmel wär'!

IV. Accentual

DIE STILLE

weiss rät keiner
wie wohl wohl
wüsst' einer einer
Mensch wissen soll

still draussen Schnee
stumm verschweigen sind
Sterne nicht Höh'
meine Gedanken sind

wünscht' wäre Morgen
fliegen Lerchen auf
überfliegen einander
Herze folgt Lauf

wünscht' wäre Vöglein
zöge über Meer
über Meer weiter
ich Himmel wär

IV. Semantic

DIE STILLE

weiss keiner wie wohl--wüsst' (es nur) einer

still, stumm, verschweigen meine Gedanken sind

wünscht' (es) wäre Morgen (da) fliegen Lerchen auf

wünscht' (ich) wäre Vöglein zöge über (das) Meer (im) Himmel

IV. Mimetic

DIE STILLE

verschweigen
Gedanken

IV. Soliloquizing

DIE STILLE

sonst

Eichendorff's "Die Stille" is an exercise in the creation of silence and secrecy. He uses meter to this end and abandons his usually predictable rhyme scheme for a more conversational and intimate style. The first strophe is the most remarkable in this regard and exhibits irregular rhythms and a mixture of poetic feet. It can be diagrammed as follows:

```
v/v/   vv/v
 /vv/v, v/
v  /vv/vv/v
v/vv/  v/
```

The irregular pace, which is at once halting and effusive, is created by the interruption of punctuation and the alternation between metrical feet which begin with an anacrusis, or unstressed syllable, and those that begin with a stressed syllable. Furthermore, the fact that some feet contain only two syllables and are thus more balanced and self-contained while others contain three syllables and feel much more unbalanced and forward moving, does much to depict the tenor of this interior monologue in which the narrator agonizes over who should know her secret.

The second and third strophes elaborate upon the young lover's emotions by comparing her thoughts to the quiet snow and the silent stars, and her desires to the extremely well-suited image of two birds darting, one over the other, as they fly together. The final strophe offers a resolution of sorts to the situation, inasmuch as we are told that the young lover will not confess her feelings to her beloved, or anyone else for that matter, but rather desires to fly off to heaven keeping her secret to herself.

Eichendorff's poem says much about the tension inherent in any secret knowledge. The essence of this tension lies in the pleasure of knowing and the fear of telling, the precarious balance between the prolongation of satisfaction and the risk of sharing that feeling and having it dissipate. The proposed resolution of this tension in the first strophe is to tell "nur einer," to share her feelings with only one other person, presumably the one with whom she is in love. Yet, as mentioned earlier, this alternative is never acted upon in the poem, rather the lover proceeds to praise and relish the feeling of secretiveness, and in the end it alone is enough to satisfy her.

Eichendorff encases the inherent tension of secrecy in the crucial seme of this poem, his use of the *subjunctive tense* and the term "*sonst*." Strophes 1, 3, and 4 are dominated by the subjunctive tense as the lover metaphorically projects her feelings onto other situations. The adjective "sonst" encapsulates her situation as she evaluates her relation to others in light of the secret.

Die Stille.

No 4.
Nicht schnell, immer sehr leise.
Es weiss und räth es doch Kei_ner, wie mir so wohl ist, so wohl! Ach!
5
wüsst' es nur Ei_ner, nur Ei_ner, kein Mensch es sonst wis_sen sollt'! So
9
still ist's nicht draussen im Schnee, so stumm und ver_schwie_gen sind die
13
Etwas lebhafter.
Ster_ne nicht in der Höh', als mei_ne Ge_danken sind.___ Ich wünscht', ich wär' ein

18
Vög - lein und zö - ge ü - ber das Meer, wohl ü - ber das Meer und weiter, bis
23
Erstes Tempo.
dass ich im Him - mel wär! Es weiss und räth' es doch Kei - ner, wie mir so wohl ist, so
28
wohl, ach! wüsst' es nur Einer, nur Ei - ner, kein Mensch es sonst wis - sen sollt', kein
33
ritard.
Mensch es sonst wis - sen sollt'.
ritard.

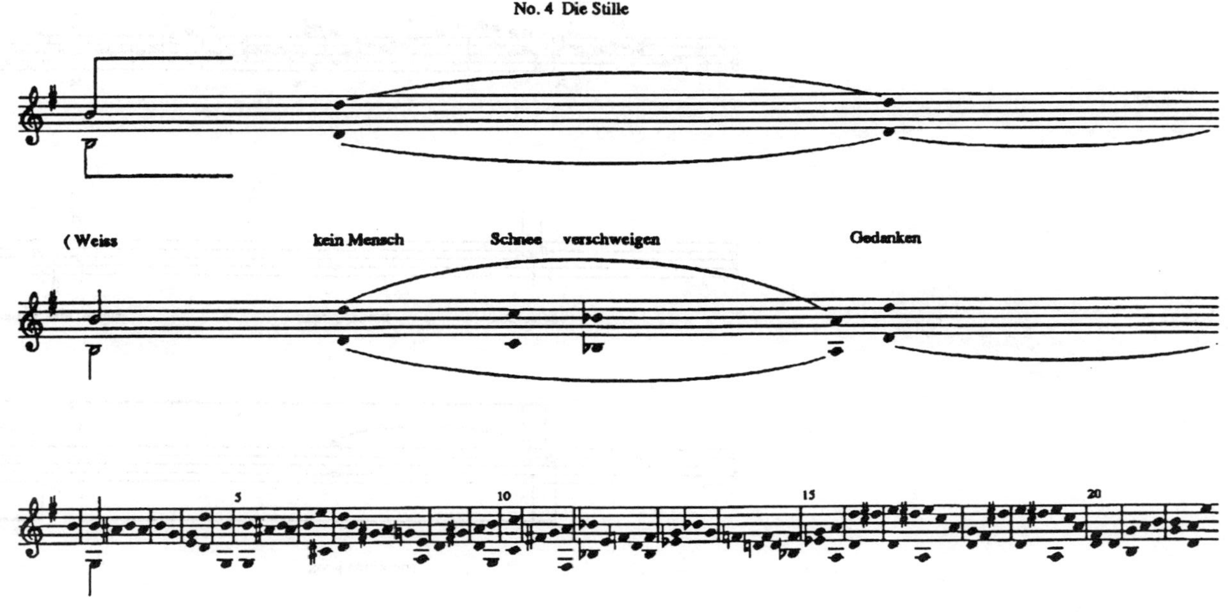
No. 4 Die Stille
(Weiss
kein Mensch
Schnee
verschweigen
Gedanken
5
10
15
20

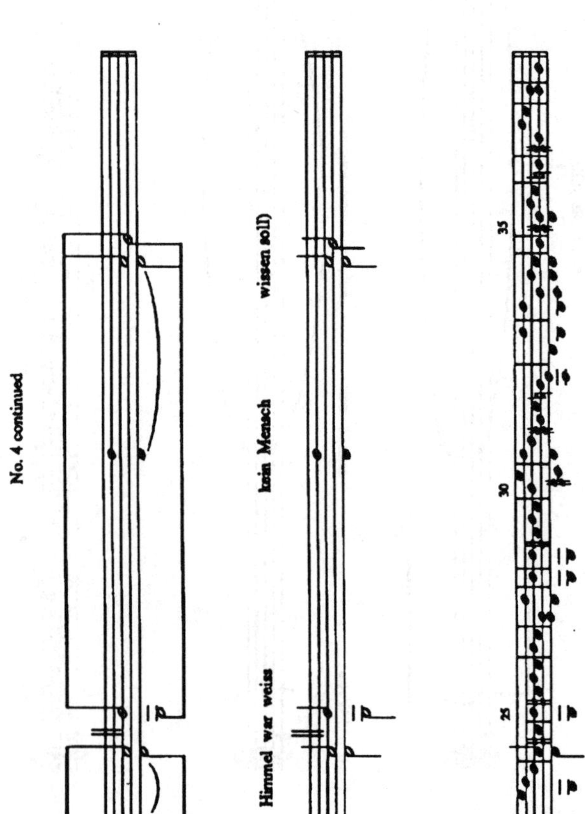
No. 4 continued
Himmel war weiss
kein Mensch
wissen soll)
25
30
35

Schumann chooses to delete the third strophe from his setting of "Die Stille." Perhaps he considered it redundant, since it is rhetorically related to the fourth strophe by its initial "Ich wünscht'." Though the image of the fourth strophe is initiated in the third, it is not dependent on the third strophe for its meaning. A more likely explanation lies in the pacing of the cycle. "Die Stille" is preceded by a relatively long setting of the poem "Waldesgespräch" and it is followed by the extremely poignant "Mondnacht"; therefore, Schumann may have desired that "Die Stille" serve the same bridging function that "Intermezzo" serves, and he may have predicted that such a function might be expected by the listener.

Eichendorff's poem made use of grammatical considerations in expressing the tension involved in secrecy. Schumann uses harmonic means to convey the same feeling. Just as Eichendorff used the subjunctive tense to convey the ambiguous nature of the girl's emotions, Schumann uses the diminished seventh chord to signify this feeling. The diminished seventh chord has the singular characteristic of being made up of three minor thirds, and the pitches created by these intervals allow the diminished seventh chord to modulate freely to virtually any key. Thus the chord is at once a tightly wrought pitch-configuration and a vehicle for great expression and change.

Schumann makes use of the diminished seventh chord at crucial moments in setting the poem. The first instance occurs in meas. 6 and is closely followed by another in meas. 7. These chords assist in the modulation from G major to D major, and the G# diminished seventh chord in meas. 7 hints at a tonicization of A. The text which these bars set is "Kein Mensch es sonst wissen soll."

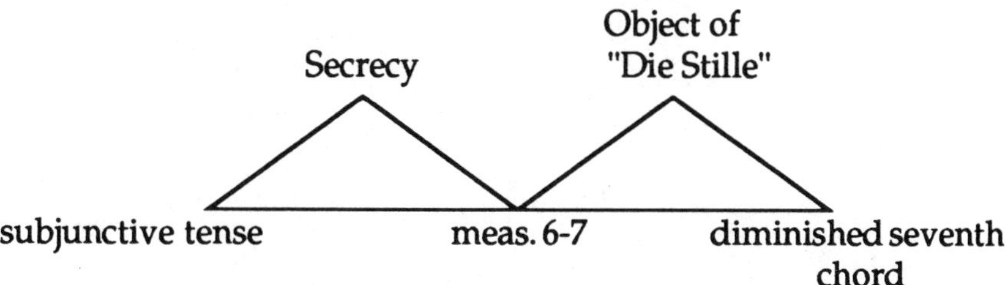

Thus Schumann chooses to use the chord which so aptly symbolizes the secret on which the poem is centered at the first and only mention of the beloved.

The *diminished seventh chord* is a musical gesture of ambiguity and unexpressed potential. Poetically speaking, potentiality is implicit in the matter of secrecy which keeps potential action in check. Potentiality is included in the poem in the vocative statements "Ich wuenscht'..." which Schumann also sets using diminished seventh chords in meas. 17 and 19. Thus the ground of the intersemiotic relationship between poem and setting in Op. 39, No. 4 is *potentiality*.

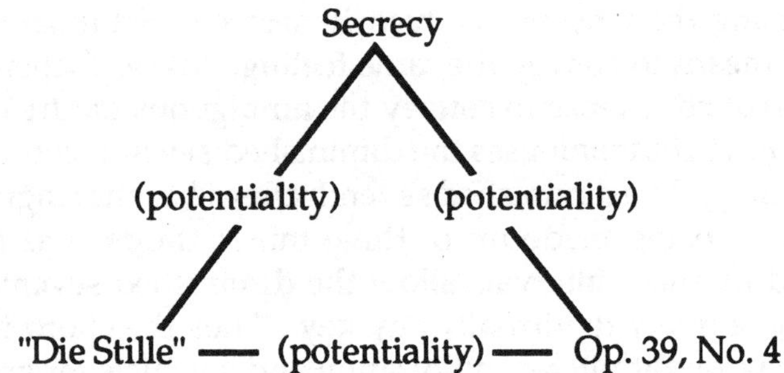

This poem comes from the *Geistliche Gedichte* section of Eichendorff's collected works. It is a metaphorical representation of the union of heaven and earth in the human soul. Schumann changes the last line of the first strophe to read "nur träumen müsst."

V. Prosodic

MONDNACHT

Es war, als hätt der Himmel
Die Erde still geküsst,
Dass sie im Blütenschimmer
Von ihm nun träumen müsst.

Die Luft ging durch die Felder,
Die Ähren wogten sacht,
Es rauschten leis die Wälder,
So sternklar war die Nacht.

Und meine Seele spannte
Weit ihre Flügel aus,
Flog durch die stillen Lande,
Als flöge sie nach Haus.

V. Accentual

MONDNACHT

war hätt Himmel
Erde still geküsst
dass Blütenschimmer
ihm träumen müsst

Luft durch Felder
Ähren wogten sacht
rauscheten leis Wälder
sternklar war Nacht

meine Seele spannte
Weit Flügel aus
Flog stillen Lande
flöge sie Haus

V. Semantic

MONDNACHT

(als) Himmel geküsst Erde, sie (von) ihm träumen müsst

meine Seele spannte, (als) flöge sie (nach) Haus

V. Mimetic

MONDNACHT

stille
leis
stillen

V. Soliloquizing

MONDNACHT

als

Certainly one of the masterpieces of nineteenth-century verse, and indeed of any era, Eichendorff's "Mondnacht" exhibits great simplicity, great balance, and multi-layered meaning. The poem is in virtually regular iambic trimeter and its images are all part of the stock of romantic verse, though they are charged with a special energy in this poem.

"Mondnacht" is about longing, the desire for union between the spiritual and the physical. It is an extremely difficult poem to explicate or paraphrase because it involves a great deal of overlapping in semiotic function. The first strophe employs heaven and earth as characters in an amorous relationship and their kiss is a sign of their desire for union. Eichendorff adds a sense of urgency to this situation in line four where we are told that earth "müsst" dream of heaven. The second strophe examines tangible manifestations of earth's response to heaven's moonlit advances. The wind, which prompts the stirring of the fields and the rustling of the forest, is the most notable of these manifestations. It is this same wind that, in the third strophe, provides the means of transport for the soul as it flies "as if" toward home. The first-person voice of the narrator which enters in the final strophe suggests that heaven and earth indeed have been united and that the experience is one of transcendence.

The essential seme in this poem is the grammatical matter of *subjunctive tense*. The quality of the subjunctive tense is its metaphoricality or its "as-if-ness" which embodies the poem's desire for union between the spiritual and the physical.

Mondnacht.
Nº 5.
Zart, heimlich.
p
Es
ritard.
7
war, als hätt' der Him - mel die Er - de still ge-küsst,
14
dass sie im Blü - thenschim - mer von ihm nur träu - men
21
müsst'.
ritard.
p
ritard.
28
p
Die Luft ging durch die Fel - der, die Äh - ren wog - ten
B.N.127.

35
nacht, es rausch - ten leis' die Wäl - der, so
41
ritard.
stern - klar war die Nacht. ritard. Und mei - ne See - le
47
spann - te weit ih - re Flü - gel aus, flog durch die
54
stil - len Lan - de, als flö - ge sie nach Haus.
61
pp
R.S.187.

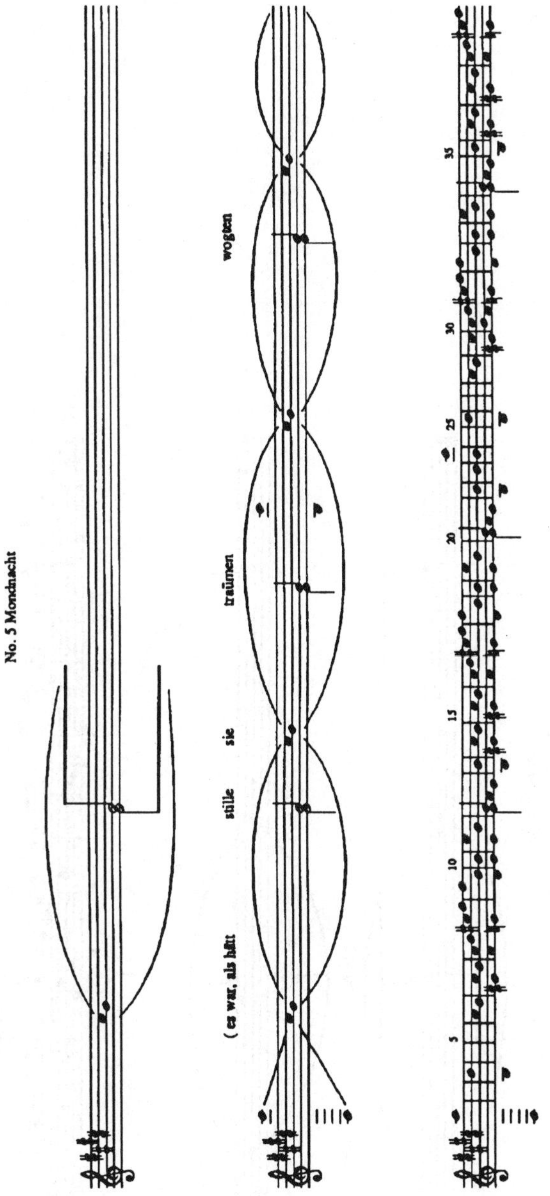
No. 5 Mondnacht
(es war, als hätt
stille
sie
traümen
wogten

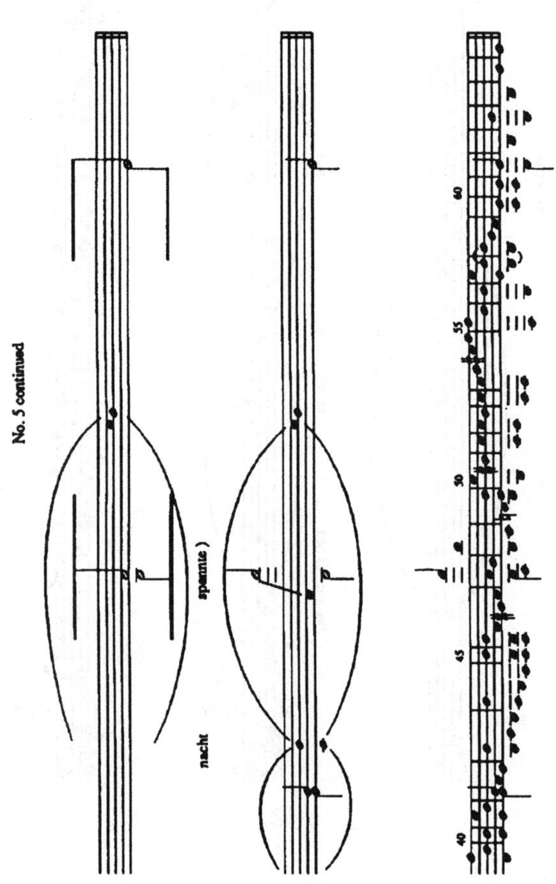
No. 5 continued
nacht
spannte)

Schumann's setting of Eichendorff's "Mondnacht" lives up to the exquisite expression of the poem in every respect. It has been suggested that Schumann's substitution of "nur" for "nun" in line four is the result of inaccurate copy-work on the part of his wife Clara (Fischer-Dieskau 1988, 76). However, this substitution adds a further suggestion of compulsion to the text by suggesting that earth must dream *only* of heaven. This setting is based upon a tension between the pitches B and C#. In addition to the harmonic function of these pitches which will be addressed below, Schumann uses them in a pictorial fashion to depict the distance between heaven and earth in meas. 1 and the union of heaven and earth in the kiss of meas. 6.

The pitches B and C# are stated together as part of two chords. In meas. 6 they are part of a B9, which is a dominant chord in E major; and in meas. 7 they are part of a C#7 which is a dominant chord in F# minor. Thus Schumann erects a musical expression filled with harmonic desire, the longing of the dominant for the tonic.

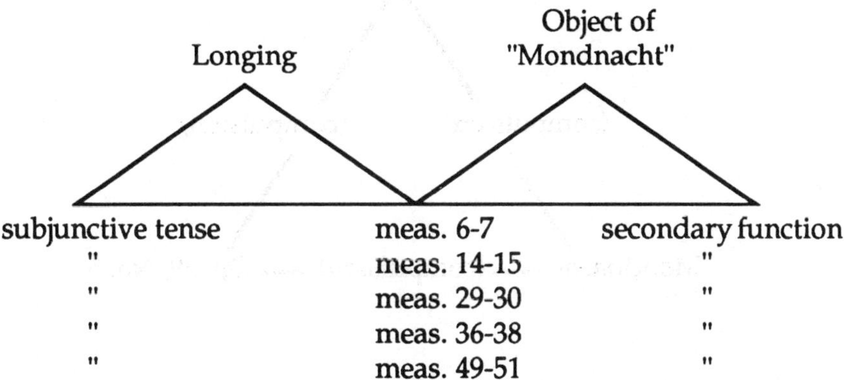

This state of harmonic longing is sustained throughout most of the composition, the tonic is rarely stated and always immediately followed by the dominant. In fact the singing of the poem ends in meas. 60 before the musical longing comes to a conclusion.

The most crucial musical gesture in the song is the use of *secondary function*, which allows Schumann to erect a compound situation of longing similar to that which exists in Eichendorff's poem. Inasmuch as secondary function involves a brief cadence in one key area in the midst of another key it is a musical metaphor, for it projects one musical idea in the midst of another and links these acoustically dissimilar expressions by way of a structural similarity. Furthermore, the progression from the dominant of the tonic to the supertonic in the key of E major is imperative to the potency of the pitch configuration B and C#.

The ground of the intersemiotic relationship between Eichendorff's poem and Schumann's setting is *compulsion*. Compulsion is represented in the poem by the metaphorical situation in which the earth "müsst" dream of heaven, and compulsion is expressed in the song by the frequent use of secondary function which necessarily involves the musical compulsion of the dominant for the tonic, of tension for resolution.

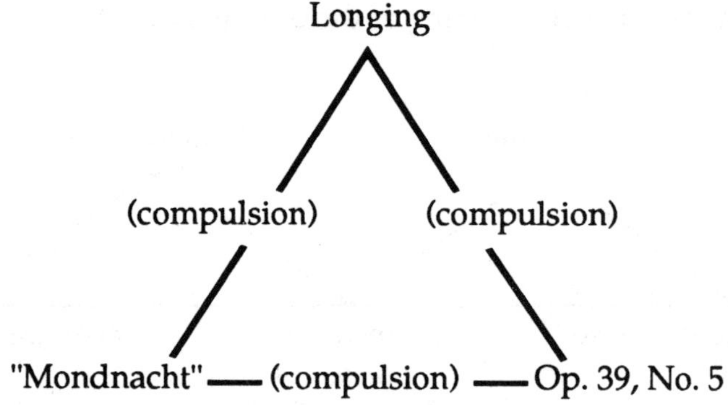

"Schöne Fremde" comes from the *Wanderlieder* section of Eichendorff's collected works. It discusses the prophetic powers of nature and the transforming powers of love.

VI. Prosodic

SCHÖNE FREMDE

Es rauschen die Wipfel und schauern,
Als machten zu dieser Stund'
Um die halbversunkenen Mauren
Die alten Götter die Rund'.

Hier hinter den Myrtenbäumen
In heimlich dämmernder Pracht
Was sprichst du wirr wie in Träumen
Zu mir, phantastische Nacht?

Es funkeln auf mich alle Sterne
Mit glühendem Liebesblick,
Es redet trunken die Ferne
Wie von künftigem, grossem Glück.

VI. Accentual

SCHÖNE FREMDE

rauschen Wipfel schauern
machten dieser Stund'
halbversunkenen Mauern
alten Götter Rund'

hinter Myrtenbäumen
heimlich dämmernder Pracht
sprichst wirr Träumen
mir phantastische Nacht

funkeln mich Sterne
glühendem Liebesblick
redet trunken Ferne
künftigem grossem Glück

VI. Semantic

SCHÖNE FREMDE

Wipfel schauern (als) machten Götter Rund'

(was) sprichst wirr (wie in) Träumen, phantastische Nacht?

Sterne (mit) glühendem Liebesblick redet künftigem grossem Glück

VI. Mimetic

SCHÖNE FREMDE

rauschen/schauern

VI. Soliloquizing

SCHÖNE FREMDE

künftigem

Eichendorff's poem is concerned with the perception of natural phenomena as supernatural phenomena in a distant location or a dream-like state. It is not stated whether this land may actually be Greece or Italy, which held such fascination for the romantics, or a part of the poet's imagination; but it seems safe to assume it is a location under the influence of love. It is populated with physical things that take on metaphysical meaning.

The objects which are a part of this metaphysical locale perform a prophetic function inasmuch as they speak of a future which is desired by the narrator. This function suggests the location of Greece, its shrines and oracles. The key to this prophetic function is the poem's crucial seme *künftigem* which lends the future-oriented temporal quality to the poem. This prophetic function is also supported by two of the objects discussed in the poem "dreams and stars" both of which are a part of the conventional means by which the future is predicted.

Schöne Fremde.
Nº 6.
Innig, bewegt.
Es rau - schen die Wi - pfel und
3
schau - ern, als mach - ten zu die - ser Stund' um die halb ver - sun - kenen
poco rit.
6
Mauern die al - ten Göt - ter die Rund'. Hier hin - ter den Myr - then -
a tempo
9
bäu - - men, in heim - lich däm - mernder Pracht, was
12
sprichst du wirr, wie in Träu - men, zu mir, phan - ta - sti - sche

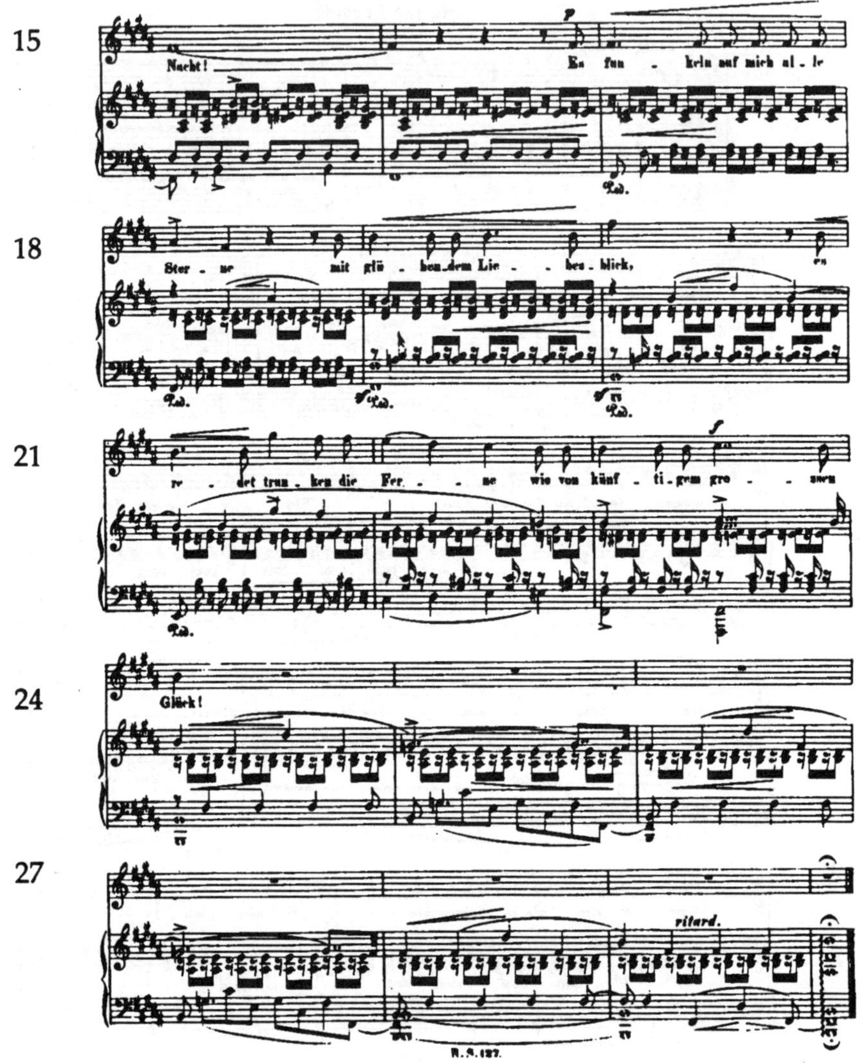
15
Nacht! Es fun - keln auf mich al - le
18
Ster - ne mit glü - hen-dem Lie - bes-blick, es
21
re - det trun - ken die Fer - ne wie von künf - ti-gem gro - ssem
24
Glück!
27
ritard.
R.S.127

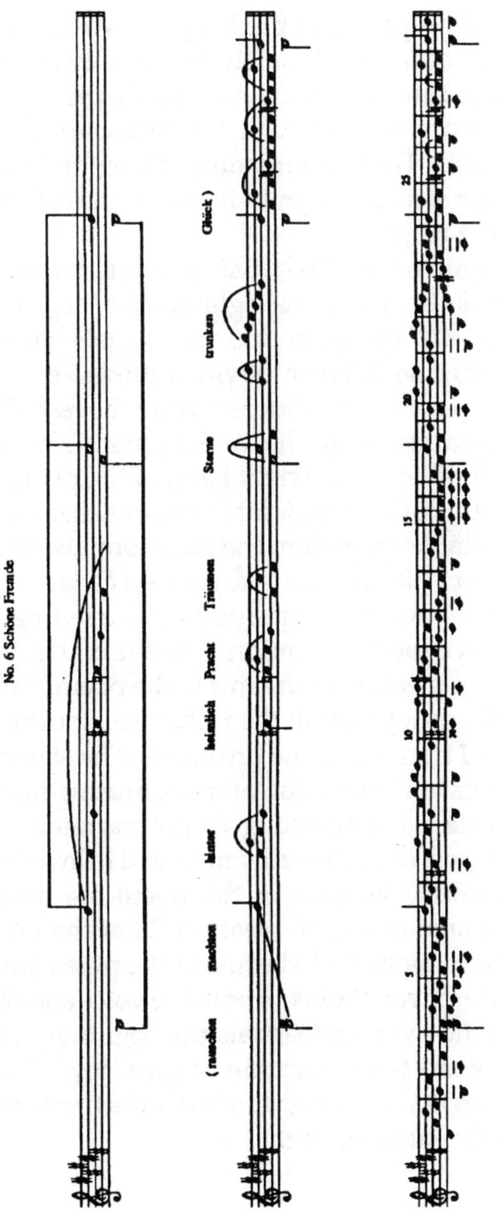
No. 6 Schöne Fremde
(rauschen
machen
hinter
heimlich
Pracht
Träumen
Sterne
trunken
Glück)
5
10
15
20
25

The matter of prophecy, or prediction, is virtually impossible to imitate in music. Music exists solely as a quality in the present and its constructions can look back and recall past musical events; however, it is extremely difficult for music to look ahead in a predictive fashion. Thus Schumann's setting of "Schöne Fremde" must use another means to signify the joyful transformation which takes place in the magical land.

Schumann symbolizes this transformation through the use of an autonomous melodic line in the right hand of the accompaniment which co-exists with the vocal line and signals harmonic motion. This autonomous line is given obvious phrase markings, and its legato character is noticeably different from the rest of the accompaniment which is rather lively. It was Schumann's common practice to double the vocal line in the right hand of the piano part, thus his departure from this procedure is all the more salient in this instance.

With one notable exception, the autonomous melodic line descends by a perfect fifth and thus suggests a cadence or moment of harmonic repose. This occurs nine times in the setting. Two of these statements deserve special attention. The use of this device in meas. 11-12 comes at the mention of dreams in the poem. The dream is, of course, a potent concept for all the romantics, for the dream transforms reality and transcends the ordinary. The statement in meas. 20-21 corresponds to the mention of the confusing manner in which the drunken distance is speaking to the narrator. This passage highlights the aspect of irrationality involved in love, in dreams, and in the way physical elements of the poem are made to assume metaphysical connotations. In meas. 21-23 of the setting the vocal line and the autonomous melodic line of the piano are in unison for the first time. Moreover, the G# in both the voice and the piano is the highest note of the piece and signals the beginning of the momentous descent toward the realization of great joy. Thus Schumann joins the two lines at this moment to show the transforming powers of dreams and the fantastic night.

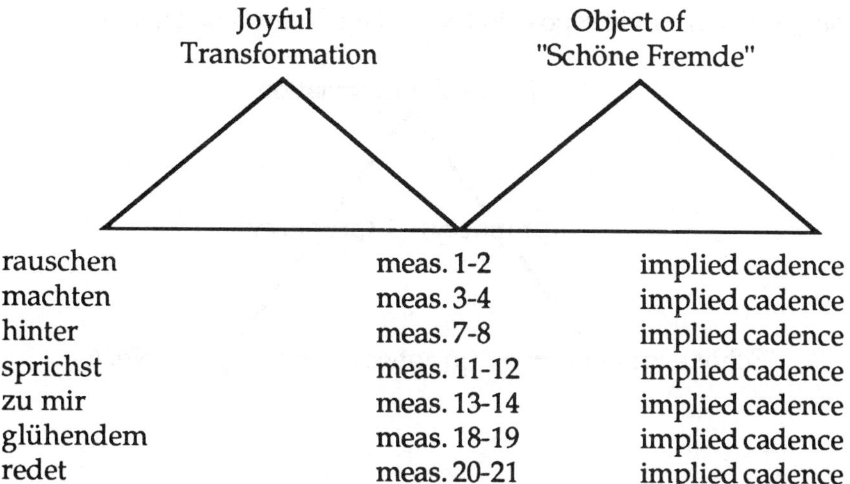

rauschen	meas. 1-2	implied cadence
machten	meas. 3-4	implied cadence
hinter	meas. 7-8	implied cadence
sprichst	meas. 11-12	implied cadence
zu mir	meas. 13-14	implied cadence
glühendem	meas. 18-19	implied cadence
redet	meas. 20-21	implied cadence

The momentous nature of meas. 21-23 and the importance of the autonomous melodic line are supported by the observation that although the accompaniment rests on a tonic triad three times in this setting, the voice never dwells on the tonic scale degree in the midst of one of these cadences until the last word of the poem, "Glück!," is sung in meas. 24. Furthermore, at the end of meas. 23 in the vocal and autonomous melodic line, Schumann makes use of the technique of anticipation, which involves the insertion of a note from a chord yet to be stated into an existent chord. This creates a momentary dissonance which, after the following chord has sounded, can be perceived as a brief anticipation of the subsequent harmonic construction.

The crucial musical gesture in this setting is the *autonomous melodic line* which suggests harmonic repose even in the midst of harmonic tension. The intersemiotic relationship in this song involves the temporal modifier "künftigem" and the autonomous melodic line as sign and interpretant of transformation. The ground of this intersemiotic relationship is *prophecy*. Prophecy is involved in the poem in its reference to the "phantastische Nacht" during which all of the transformations take place. The setting expresses the conception of prophecy in the autonomous melodic line which suggests harmonic repose in the midst of harmonic tension.

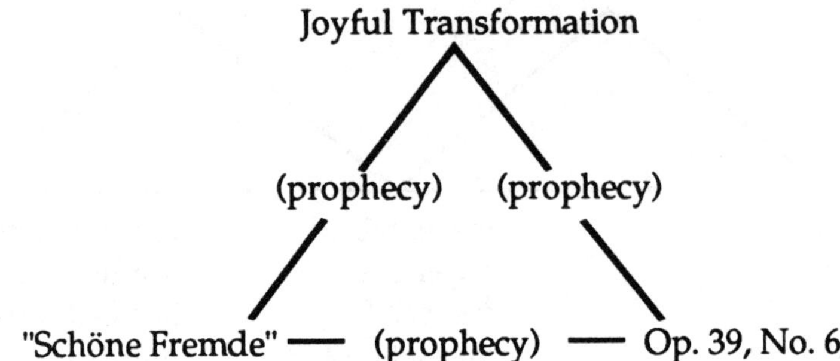

"Auf einer Burg" is also taken from the *Wanderlieder* section of Eichendorff's collected works. It is a poem which associates images of the past with those of the present in an unexpected manner.

VII. Prosodic

AUF EINER BURG

Eingeschlafen auf der Lauer
Oben ist der alte Ritter;
Drüben gehen Regenschauer
Und der Wald rauscht durch das Gitter.

Eingewachsen Bart und Haare
Und versteinert Brust und Krause,
Sitzt er viele hundert Jahre
Oben in der stillen Klause.

Draussen ist es still und friedlich
Alle sind ins Tal gezogen,
Waldesvögel einsam singen
In den leeren Fensterbogen.

Eine Hochzeit fährt da unten
Auf dem Rhein im Sonnenscheine,
Musikanten spielen munter,
Und die schöne Braut, die weinet.

VII. Accentual

AUF EINER BURG

eingeschlafen auf Lauer
oben ist alte Ritter
drüben gehen Regenschauer
Wald rauscht Gitter

eingewachsen Bart Haare
versteinert Brust Krause
sitzt viele hundert Jahre
oben stillen Klause

draussen ist still freidlich
alle sind Tal gezogen
Waldesvögel einsam singen
leeren Fensterbogen

Hochzeit fährt unten
Rhein Sonnenscheine
Musikanten spielen munter
schöne Braut weinet

VII. Semantic

AUF EINER BURG

eingeschlafen (ist) Ritter (und) Wald (durch das) Gitter

versteinert sitzt (in) stillen Klause

draussen ist still friedlich, Waldesvogel einsam singen

Hochzeit fährt unten, schöne Braut (die) weinet

VII. Mimetic

AUF EINER BURG

eingeschlafen
versteinert
einsam
weinet

VII. Soliloquizing

AUF EINER BURG

ein...

At first reading, Eichendorff's "Auf einer Burg" can prove puzzling. It is filled with seemingly unrelated images described in cryptic phrases, all of which tend to merge together into an amorphous and ambiguous whole. The feeling conveyed seems to one of great melancholy and solitude, however the means by which this emotion is presented are unconventional, especially in regard to the final line of the poem in which the weeping bride is out of place. Yet this is a moving poem, it is well crafted, and every expression contributes to a unified theme of isolation.

Eichendorff creates both the setting for, and the feeling of, isolation by using a progression of images in the first three strophes. All of these images refer to the old knight and the castle. Each sign of isolation involves a distance from experience: sleep places an unconscious screen between the individual and reality, petrification places a physiological barrier between the individual and reality, and loneliness places a psychological barrier between the individual and reality. Each of the poetic interpretants of these signs of isolation grasp the sign in terms of a physical analogy: sleep is like a grating which separates the individual from reality, age is like a prison cell which detains a person from experiencing reality, and loneliness is like the empty window which deters a person from reality.

Eichendorff links all of these signs of isolation together by way of assonance. "Eingeschlafen," "Eingewachsen," and "einsam singen" share the syllable "ein" which, in itself, speaks of isolation and singularity. It is this matter of assonance which then allows Eichendorff to make the seemingly illogical leap from the images of the knight to the image of the weeping bride. The fourth strophe is literally singing with the assonant syllable *ein* which is the crucial seme of the poem. It is present in the terms: eine, Rhein, Sonnenscheine, and most importantly in the term "weinet" upon which the poem hinges. Thus Eichendorff points the critical attitude of the reader toward an understanding of the poem and the image of the weeping bride in terms of the feeling of a premonition of death in the midst of life which is a part of the romantic psyche.

The last strophe is also remarkable for the fact that three of the four lines are end-stopped, which deviates from the practice in the rest of the poem. This serves to emphasize the happiness and vibrancy of each of the images of the fourth strophe in opposition to the rest of the poem. Furthermore, the comma after "Braut" in the last line of the poem creates a great deal of expectation and does much to contribute to the poignancy of the moment.

Nº 7.
Auf einer Burg.
Adagio.
p
Ein_ge_schla_fen auf der Lau_er o_ben ist der al_te Rit_ter, drü_ben ge_hen
6
Re_gen_schau_er und der Wald rauscht durch das Git_ter, Ein_ge_wach_sen Bart und Haa_re
11
und ver_stei_nert Brust und Krau_se, sitzt er vie_le hun_dert Jah_re o_ben in der stil_len
17
Klau_se. Draussen ist es still und friedlich, al_le sind in's
25
Thal ge_zo_gen, Wal_des_vö_gel ein_sam sin_gen in den lee_ren Fen_ster_bo_gen.
R.S.127.

30
Ei - ne Hoch - zeit fährt da un - ten auf dem Rhein im Son - nen - schei - ne,
34
ritard.
Mu - si - kan - ten spie - len mun - ter, und die schö - ne Braut, die wei - - net.
ritard.

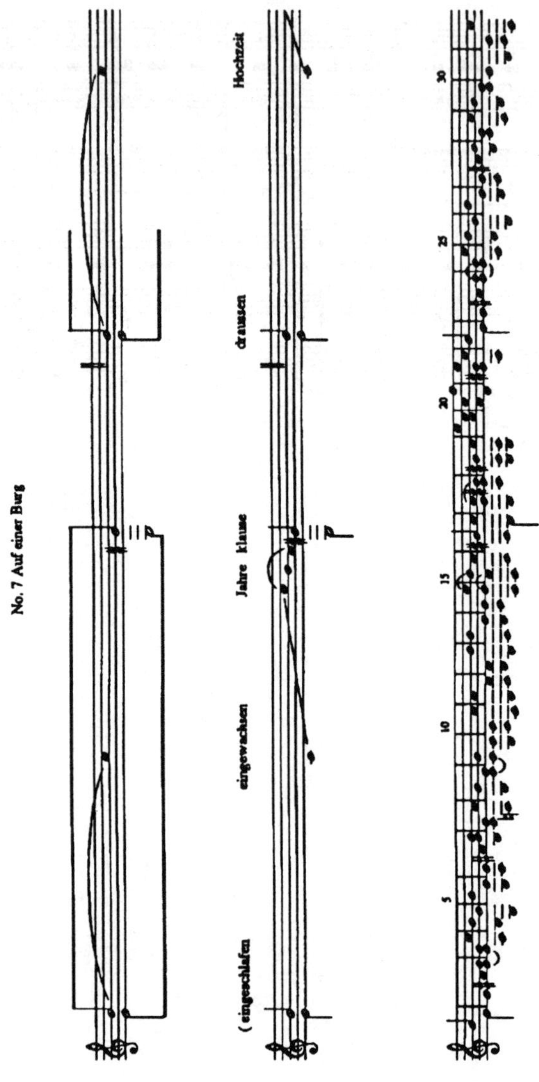
No. 7 Auf einer Burg
(eingeschlafen
eingewachsen
Jahre klause
draussen
Hochzeit
5
10
15
20
25
30

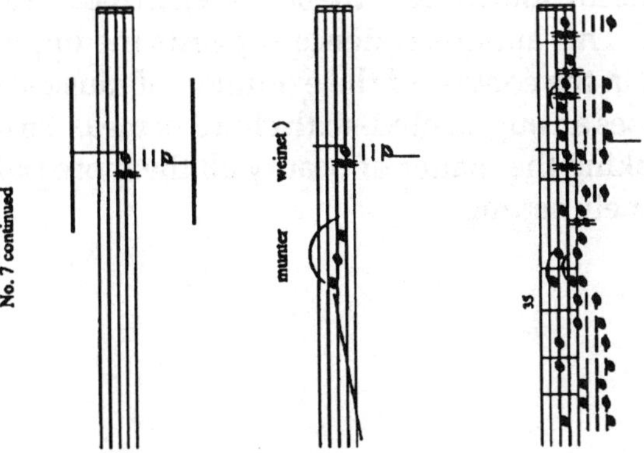
No. 7 continued
munter
weinet)
35

Upon first hearing, Schumann's song is as mysterious and enigmatic as the poem which it sets. It is obvious that he fully grasped the meaning of the poem and the manner in which it functioned. Schumann treats Eichendorff's poem as if it were made up of two rather than four strophes. As a result the portions of the poem which refer to aging and the playing of music are set with the same sequential passage. Furthermore, this design dictates that the mention of the weeping bride is set with the same music that is used to accompany the description of the silent cell where the old knight sits.

The most immediate question the music provokes is one of tonality versus modality. Judging from the key signature and the antique sounding polyphonic texture, the song seems to be in the Phrygian mode. Yet the presence of the pitch F# in the first bars and its frequent use throughout the composition suggests E minor. The five-note motive with which the song begins does much to re-present the isolation which is the object of the poem.  This motive depicts the inert quality described in the poem harmonically. It involves melodic motion, but it is harmonically petrified.

Schumann also makes use of the device of sequence to re-present the process of aging. By setting the terms "eingewachsen" and "versteinert" in the midst of a prolonged sequence, he employs a musical device which has the psychological effect of slowing time. A sequence fills the progression of musical time with the same intervals stated at different pitch levels. It involves the presence of predictable repetition in the midst of temporal progression, which is indeed an aspect of biological aging. Schumann uses a Phrygian cadence at the mention of both the silent cell in meas. 16 and the bride in meas. 37. This antique cadence suggests the opposition of past and present in the context of the evolution of musical styles. Schumann also uses an augmented-sixth chord in meas. 36 to set the term "schöne" making the matter of beauty all the more poignant in this stark and lonely setting.

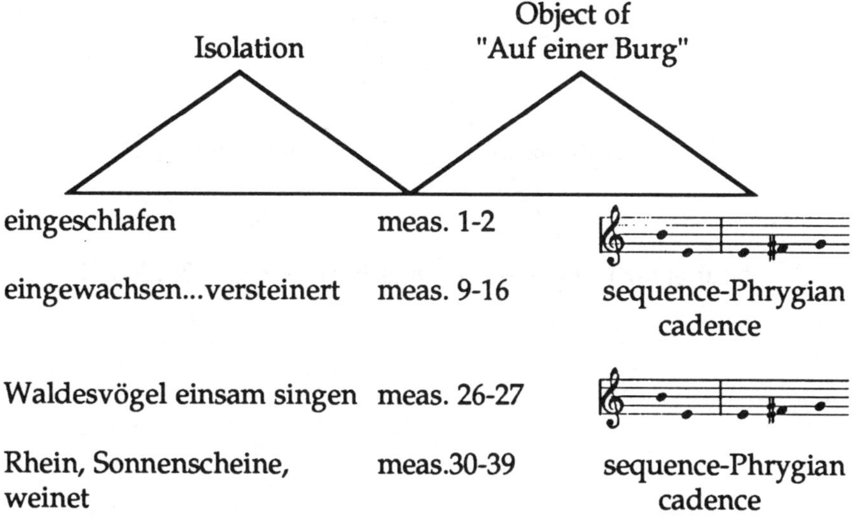

In virtually every portion of this setting which has been discussed above, the single pitch F and its chromatic alteration plays a crucial role. It is the use of F# instead of F in the opening bars which suggests E minor instead of the phrygian mode. Conversely, the use of F instead of F# creates the half-step relationship which is crucial to the Phrygian cadences of meas. 16 and 37. Thirdly, the pitch F is the lowest sounding pitch in the augmented-sixth chord of meas. 36 which is used to set the term "schöne." Thus Schumann's use of one pitch to perform a number of different functions, all of which contribute to a unified musical expression, is not unlike the role of the syllable and term "ein" in Eichendorff's poem.

The intersemiotic relationship at work in this song involves the syllable and term "ein" and *the pitch F and its chromatic alteration* as sign and interpretant of the poetic content of isolation. The ground of the relation between this poem and its setting is *alienation*. Alienation, the result of isolation, is included in the poem's description of the old knight and alienation is expressed in the song through both the tonal and modal uses of the pitch F and its chromatic alterations.

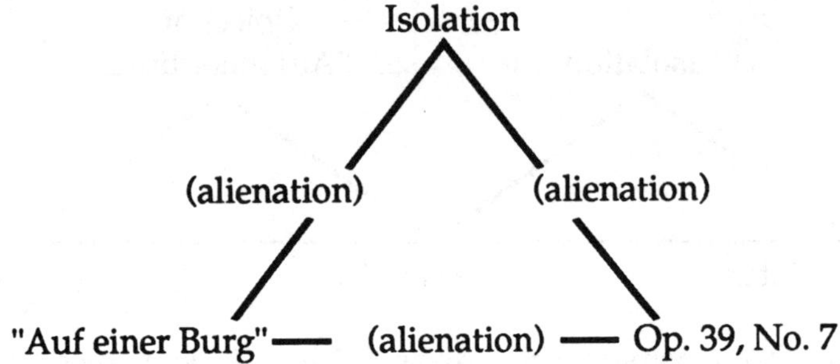
Isolation
(alienation)
(alienation)
"Auf einer Burg"
(alienation)
Op. 39, No. 7

This poem also comes from the *Wanderlieder* section of Eichendorff's collected works. In Schumann's setting, line eight reads "Von der alten schönen Zeit," line thirteen reads "in dem Garten," and line fifteen reads "Meine Liebste." One of his three repetitions of the final line reads "Und ist doch so lange tot."

VIII. Prosodic

ERINNERUNG

Ich hör' die Bächlein rauschen
Im Walde her und hin.
Im Walde, in dem Rauschen,
Ich weiss nicht, wo ich bin.

Die Nachtigallen schlagen
Hier in der Einsamkeit,
Als wollten sie was sagen
Von alter, schöner Zeit.

Die Mondesschimmer fliegen,
Als säh' ich unter mir
Das Schloss im Tale liegen,
Und ist doch so weit von hier!

Als müsste in den Garten,
Voll Rosen weiss und rot,
Mein' Liebste auf mich warten,
Und ist doch lange tot.

VIII. Accentual

ERINNERUNG

hör' Bächlein rauschen
Walde her hin
Walde in Rauschen
weiss (nicht) wo bin

Nachtigallen schlagen
Hier (in) Einsamkeit
wollten sie sagen
alter schöner Zeit

Mondesschimmer fliegen
säh' unter mir
Schloss Tale liegen
doch weit hier

müsste in Garten
Rosen weiss rot
Liebste auf warten
ist doch lange tot

VIII. Semantic

ERINNERUNG

rauschen (im) Walde, (im) Walde Rauschen

Nachtigallen schlagen (als) sagen (von) alter schöner Zeit

Mondesschimmer fliegen (als) säh' (ich) Schloss

(als) müsste Liebste warten, (ist) doch lange tot

VIII. Mimetic

ERINNERUNG

rauschen-Rauschen
weiss-weiss

VIII.Soliloquizing

ERINNERUNG

ist doch lange tot

The past to which the images of "Erinnerung" are connected is specifically a poetic past. Although Schumann chose and ordered the poems in this cycle, the recycling of poetic images is an Eichendorffian characteristic. The most obvious connections to the poetic past of the song cycle are the image of the rustling forest (Op. 39, No. 6), the statement "wo ich bin" (Op. 39, No. 3), the bird singing in solitude (Op. 39, No. 7), the notion of "alter, schöne Zeit" (Op. 39, No. 2), the image of the castle (Op. 39, Nos. 3 and 7), and the statement "ist lange tot" (Op. 39, No. 1).

This poem is concerned with the manner in which memory can confuse perception and it thrives upon the way memory influences our interpretation of the objects and experiences we encounter. Each image in this poem has significance within the closed system of the poetic statement; however, the significance of many of the images is augmented and/or modified by the way that image is used in other poetic expressions. This expansion of the semiotic powers of the representamen and the grasping of its meaning both within and outside of the immediate sphere of its use are at the heart of Peirce's triadic model of signification and his theory of the interpretant.

A good example of this situation is seen in the image of the rustling forest. As will be recalled, the notion of "rauschen" was used in the poem "Schöne Fremde" Op. 39, No. 6 to signify the relation between the rustling forest and the old gods; thus it signified the manner in which actual events took on metaphysical significance in the distant land of the poem. The notion of "rauschen" is used in "Erinnerung" to signify memory's confusion of perception by imitating the way sounds in the forest can cause a person to become lost. The fact that Eichendorff repeats the term in a varied form in "Erinnerung" reinforces this meaning in an iconic sense and adds to the state of confusion being described. The first mention of "rauschen" uses the term as a verb to describe the action of a brook, while the second use is as a noun. The important signs of memory's confusion of perception are the verbs used at the end of the odd-numbered lines of the first three strophes. As was the case in "Auf einer Burg," this poem creates a relationship among a group of images and then makes use of the meaning of this relationship in a striking manner in the final strophe. In the case of "Auf einer Burg" the meaning of the relationship was isolation, and it was imposed upon the bride celebrating her wedding day. In the case of "Erinnerung" the meaning of the relationship is confusion, and it is imposed upon the memory of the beloved who is described in the final line of the poem as "long since dead."

The fact that all of the images of the first three strophes have been transformed by memory into wondrous and positive things creates the expectation that this same transformation will take place in the fourth strophe. When the image of the beloved occurs this expectation is dashed by the intrusion of the fact that she is already dead. Eichendorff achieves such a poignant moment by waiting until the very last line to give the reader the salient information, much as he waits until the very last line of "Auf einer Burg" to mention the weeping bride.

The crucial seme in this poem is the conjunction *doch.* It signals the undeniable intrusion of present fact which memory cannot confuse. This term halts the progression of images displayed in the first three strophes. "Doch" is first used in the final line of the third strophe where it is the last part of an anapestic foot and receives stress. In the final line of the fourth strophe either "ist" or "doch" may be stressed. The prevailing pattern of the poem suggests that the verb should be emphasized in the last line, yet the other use of the conjunction suggests that it should be stressed in this instance. The result is that both terms receive stress in the mind of the reader which highlights the demise of the beloved as a present and bitter truth over and against the reverie of memory.

In der Fremde.

14
18
23
28
33
ritard.
Im
woll - ten sie was sa - gen von der al - ten schö - nen Zeit! Die
Im
Tempo.
Mon - desschimmer flie - gen, als säh' ich un - ter mir das Schloss im Tha - le
lie - gen, und ist doch so weit von hier! Als müss - te in dem Gar - ten voll
Ro - sen weiss und roth meine Lieb - ste auf mich war - ten, und ist doch so lan - ge
todt, und ist doch lan - ge todt, und ist doch lan - ge todt.
R.S.187.

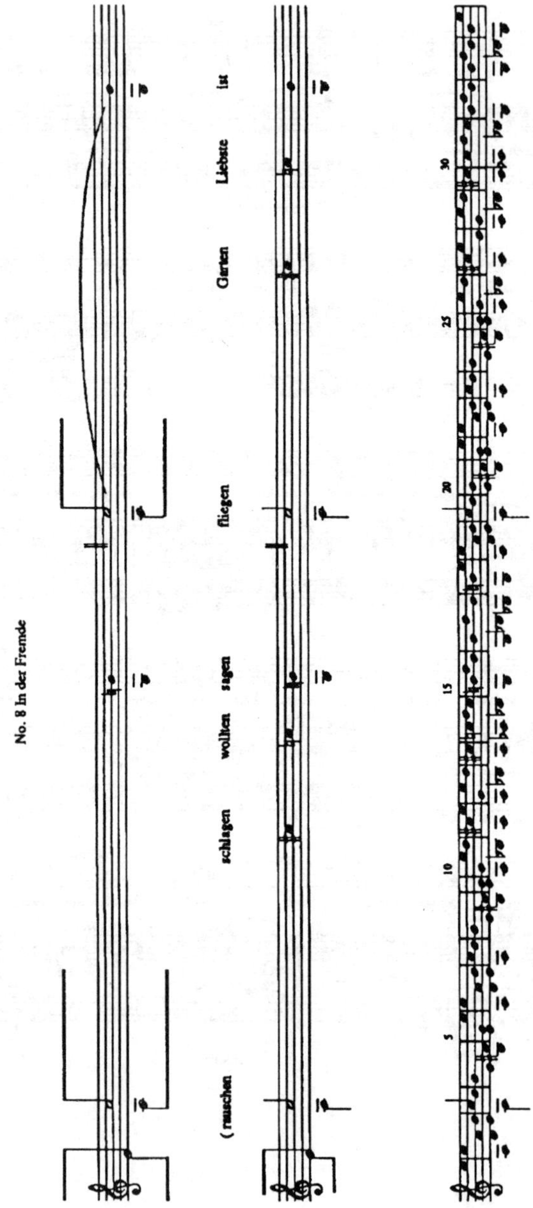
No. 8 In der Fremde
(rauschen
schlagen
wollten
sagen
fliegen
Garten
Liebste
ist

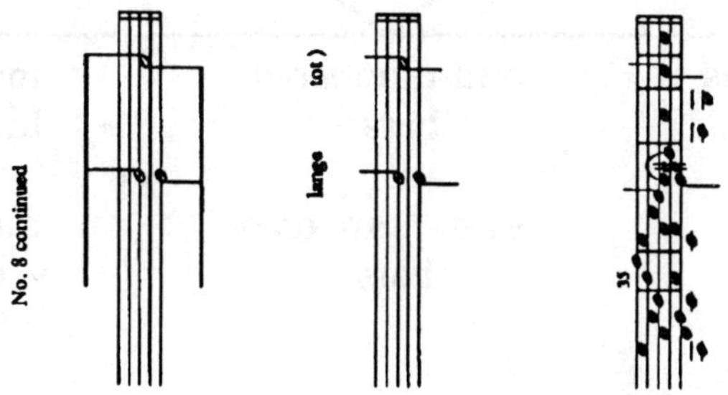
No. 8 continued
lange
tot)
35

The priorities with which Schumann approaches "Erinnerung" seem to be centered upon emphasizing the connections between this poem and the rest of the cycle. To this end, Schumann changes the title of the song to "In der Fremde" to highlight its relation to Op. 39, Nos. 1 and 7. Furthermore, he connects the piece harmonically to Op. 39, No. 7. It can be argued that Schumann's setting of "Auf einer Burg" ends with a half-cadence in the key of A minor, yet the song began in either E minor or the Phrygian mode. The first bar of his setting of "In der Fremde" centers on E, thus the first bar of Op. 39, No. 7 can be heard as a final cadence to Op. 39, No. 6, a point which argues strongly against the practice of free transposition which is common in the performance of this cycle.

In this setting, Schumann makes use of an opposition between linear and vertical musical elements to re-present the confusion which is the object of Eichendorff's poem. The odd-numbered bars contain an exceptionally pictorial figure which embodies the activity suggested by the verbs at the end of almost every odd-numbered line in the poem. The even-numbered bars are more vertically oriented and many of them include exact quotations of the melodic theme of isolation from Op. 39, No. 7. Thus Schumann uses elements of melody to depict the fanciful memories of the narrator and the element of harmony, coupled with the quotation from the previous song, to depict the intrusion of fact.

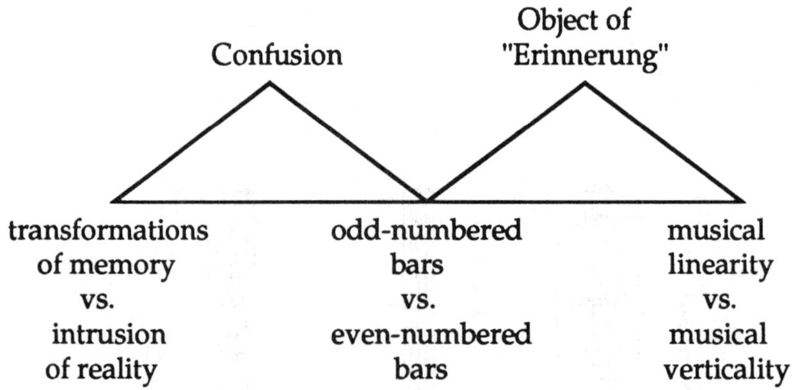

This *juxtaposition of musical elements,* which is the crucial musical gesture of the setting, plays the same role in the song as the conjunction "doch" does in the Eichendorff's "Erinnerung." The ground of the relation between poem and setting is *disparateness.* Disparateness is poetically depicted by the distance, or gulf, which exist between perception and reality, and it is included in the poem's terms "weit" and "lange" which express spatial and temporal removal. Disparateness is expressed in the opposition of linear and vertical musical elements in the odd and even-numbered bars of the setting.

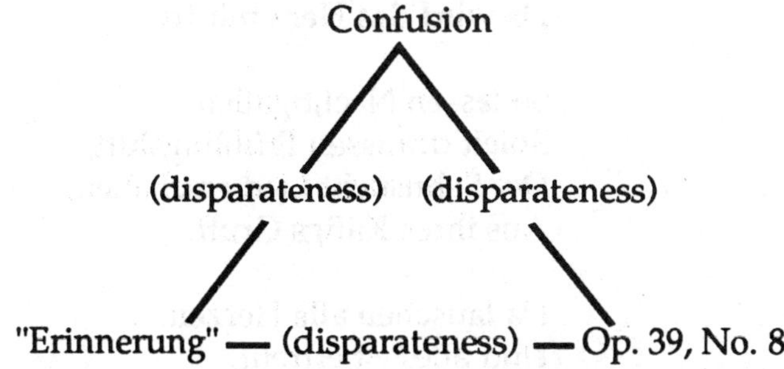

The poem "Wehmut" is from the *Sängerleben* section of Eichendorff's collected works. It is a meditation on melancholia. Schumann changes the second strophe to begin with "es lassen" and end with "Aus ihres Kerkers Gruft."

IX. Prosodic

WEHMUT

Ich kann wohl manchmal singen,
Als ob ich fröhlich sei,
Doch heimlich Tränen dringen,
Da wird das Herz mir frei.

So lassen Nachtigallen,
Spielt draussen Frühlingsluft,
Der Sehnsucht Lied erschallen,
Aus ihres Käfigs Gruft.

Da lauschen alle Herzen,
Und alles ist erfreut,
Doch keiner fühlt die Schmerzen,
Im Lied das tiefe Leid.

IX. Accentual

WEHMUT

kann manchmal singen
ob fröhlich sei
heimlich Tränen dringen
wird Herz frei

lassen Nachtigallen
draussen Frühlingsluft
Sehnsucht Lied erschallen
ihres Käfigs Gruft

lauschen alle Herzen
alles ist erfreut
keiner fühlt Schmerzen
Lied tiefe Leid

IX. Semantic

WEHMUT

manchmal singen (als ob) fröhlich, (doch) heimlich Tränen dringen

lassen Nachtigallen, Sehnsucht Lied erschallen

keiner fühlt Lied tiefe Leid

IX. Mimetic

WEHMUT

(every line is end-stopped)

IX. Soliloquizing

WEHMUT

Lied-Leid

Eichendorff's "Wehmut" addresses the disparity between appearance and reality in a state of melancholy. The emotional concept of melancholy received a great deal of attention in the nineteenth century from both psychological and aesthetic perspectives. The aspect of melancholy which occupies Eichendorff is the manner in which that state of mind is perpetuated by the perception of a gulf between appearance and fact.

The poem examines the disparity between the pleasant aural sensation of hearing a song and the depressive effect singing may have upon the singer. Eichendorff signifies this relation between sensual pleasure and spiritual pain by employing a series of terms which exhibit a combination of acoustic similarity and semantic opposition. Although there are no literal homonyms in this poem, the relation between these terms is homonym-like. Examples of this homonym-like relation include:

ich fröhlich - doch heimlich
ich singen - Tränen dringen
Frühlingsluft - Käfigs Gruft
Herzen - Schmerzen
Lied - Leid

The most striking of these pairs of terms is Lied-Leid which occurs in the last line of the poem. Here Eichendorff states the theme of the poem and the most potent example of its aesthetic impact in the same phrase. Furthermore, he makes the statement through the use of the two terms which come the closest to being actual homonyms. The disparity between "Lied" and "Leid" encapsulates the disparity between the pleasant sound of the song and the melancholy attitude of the performer. Thus the crucial seme of the poem is the *homonym-like function* of the terms discussed above, especially as that relation exists in "Lied" and "Leid."

No. 9.
Wehmuth.
Sehr langsam.
sehr gebunden
Ich kann wohl manch-mal sin-gen, als ob ich fröh-lich sei; doch
6
heimlich Thrä-nen drin-gen, da wird das Herz mir frei. Es las-sen Nachti-gal-len,
12
spielt draussen Frühlingsluft, der Sehn-sucht Lied er-schal-len aus ih-res Ker-kers
ritard.
17
Gruft. Da lauschen al-le Her-zen, und Alles ist er-freut, doch Kei-ner fühlt die
23
Schmerzen, im Lied das tie-fe Leid.
ritard.

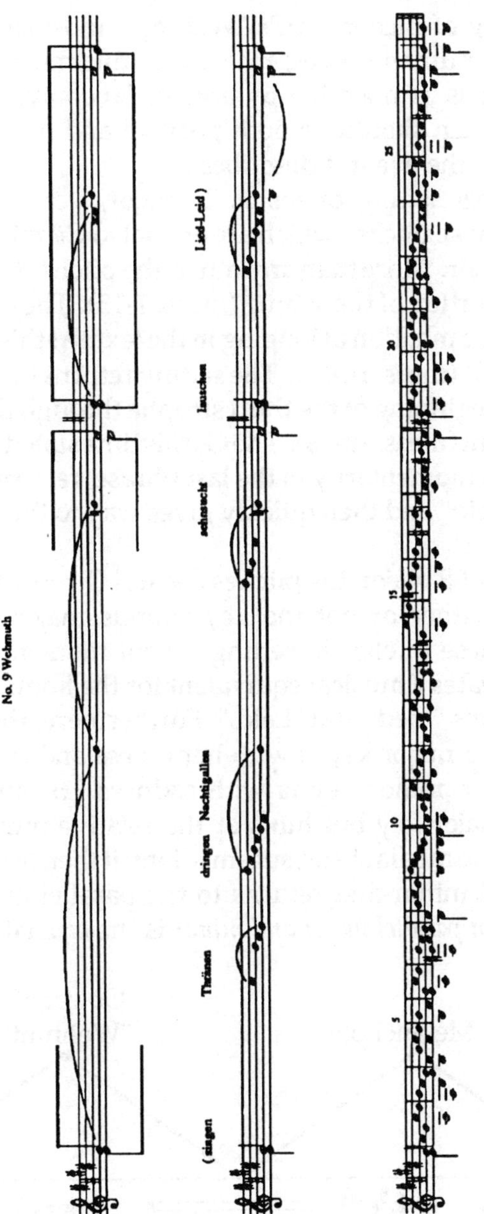
No. 9 Wehmuth
(singen
Thränen
dringen
Nachtigallen
sehnsucht
lauschen
Lied-Leid)

The setting of Eichendorff's "Wehmut" most certainly posed a challenge to Schumann. In essence, the setting must be a song about a song which is at once happy and melancholy; it is an artistic expression which should be both positive and negative, and once removed from the event it describes.

Schumann's setting opens in E major, yet the melodic line emphasizes those pitches which are crucial to C# minor, the relative minor of E major. More than any other, the pitch G# is prolonged in the opening portion of the setting (meas. 1-13). The emphasis on G# gives way at the mention of longing in the text. At this point the pitch prolonged is G (meas. 14-17). The setting returns to its emphasis on G# from the beginning of the third strophe through the penultimate line of the poem (meas. 18-23). The G, this time stated as an F double-sharp, returns momentarily in the last phrase, referring to the terms "Lied" and "Leid" and then quickly gives way to the G# in meas. 25 to the end.

In the key of E major, the pitches G# and G, more than any other, determine whether or not the key sounds major or minor. By contrasting these pitches in setting salient moments in the poem, Schumann creates a musical equivalent for the homonym-like function of the terms "Lied" and "Leid." Furthermore, the conventional association of a major key is with happiness and the conventional association of a minor key is with sadness. Schumann's setting begins in a major key but hints at the relative minor through its emphasis on the mediant and sub-mediant; it then briefly modulates to the parallel minor and returns to the parallel major. Thus the *relation between parallel major and minor* is the crucial gesture of this poem.

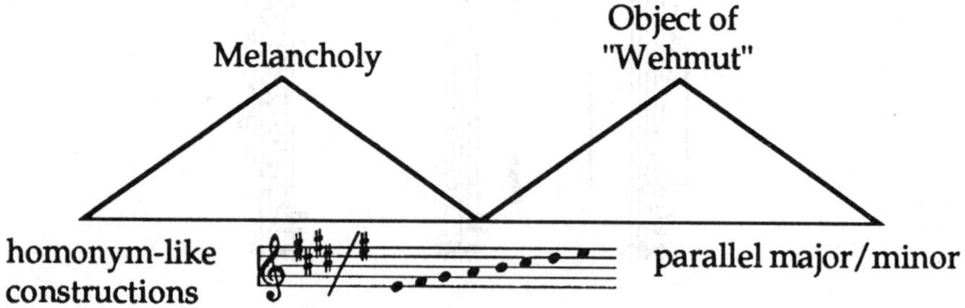

The intersemiotic relationship in Op. 39, No. 9 is one in which the homonym-like constructions and the relation between E major/E minor serve as sign and interpretant of the melancholy dichotomy between sound and sensation. The ground of this relation is *variability*. Variability is included in the poem in the term "manchmal" and the juxtaposition of the song with the experience of the singer. Variability is included in the setting in the variable relation between E major, its parallel minor, and its relative minor.

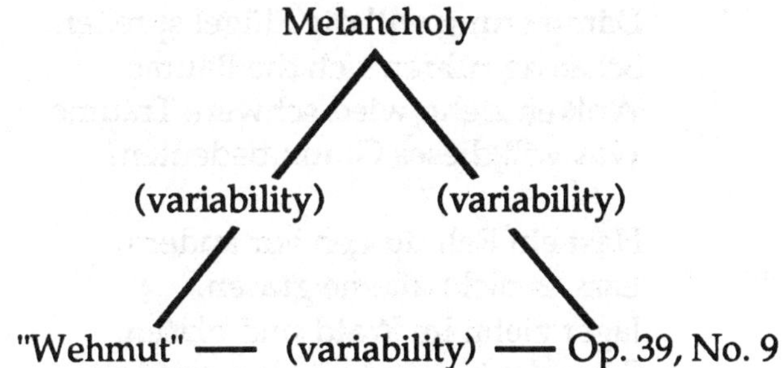

The tenth poem in this cycle is from the *Wanderlieder* section of Eichendorff's collected works. It examines twilight and its inherent dangers. Schumann changes line thirteen to read "Was heut' gehet müde unter." In line fifteen "bleibt" is changed to "geht" and in line sixteen "bleib" reads "sei."

X. Prosodic

ZWIELICHT

Dämmerung will die Flügel spreiten,
Schaurig rühren sich die Bäume,
Wolken ziehn wied schwere Träume
Was will dieses Graun bedeuten?

Hast ein Reh du lieb vor andern,
Lass es nicht alleine grasen,
Jäger ziehn im Wald und blasen,
Stimmen hin und wieder wandern.

Hast du einen Freund hienieden,
Trau ihm nicht zu dieser Stunde,
Freundlich wohl mit Aug' und Munde,
Sinnt er Krieg im tück'schen Frieden.

Was heut müde gehet unter,
Hebt sich morgen neugeboren,
Manches bleibt in Nacht verloren
Hüte dich, bleib wach und munter!

X. Accentual

ZWIELICHT

Dämmerung will Flügel spreiten
Schaurig rühren sich Bäume
Wolken ziehn schwere Träume
was dieses Graun bedeuten

hast Reh lieb andern
lass nicht alleine grasen
Jäger ziehn Wald blasen
Stimmen hin wieder wandern

hast einen Freund hienieden
trau nicht dieser Stunde
freundlich wohl Aug' Munde
Sinnt Krieg tück'schen Frieden

was müde gehet unter
hebt morgen neugeboren
manches bleibt Nacht verloren
hüte dich wach munter

X. Semantic

ZWIELICHT

Dämmerung--Was will bedeuten?

Reh--lass nicht alleine grasen

Freund--trau nicht dieser Stunde

Hüte dich wach munter

X. Mimetic

ZWIELICHT

(imperative mood)

X. Soliloquizing

ZWIELICHT

was will dieses Graun bedeuten?

Eichendorff's "Zwielicht" examines feelings of puzzlement and disturbance. By placing this poem immediately following "Wehmut" Schumann does much to steer the reader/listener toward a correct understanding of the poem; for like "Wehmut" this poem is concerned with matters of perception and ambiguity.

Twilight, which is the topic of this poem, has long been associated with supernatural occurrences, and it is the way this time of day transforms otherwise commonplace and attractive images into threatening omens which is the object of the poem. The first sign used by Eichendorff to stand for this ominous transformation is the indistinct sound of the hunting horns, a sound which is at once an evocative romantic image of the beauty of nature and a literal sign of a dangerous hunt in progress. Such a use of the sound of the horn is characteristic of Eichendorff, indeed it has been encountered in previous poems in this cycle and will be used in subsequent ones. The other sign used to stand for the ominous transformations of twilight is the smiling face of a friend which, Eichendorff warns, masks malicious intentions.

The poem ends with an admonition to beware of the ambiguous nature of outwardly attractive situations. This admonition takes the form of a kind of truth statement, "was heut müde gehet unter/ hebt sich morgen neugeboren," which is followed by an observation filled with menacing innuendo "manches bleibt in Nacht verloren." The final line of the poem warns the reader "Hüte dich, bleib wach und munter!" This statement is related to the two signs of ominous transformation discussed above by the *imperative mood* which it shares with lines 6 and 10 and is the crucial seme of the poem. Much of the ambiguous tone of this poem is derived from these imperative statements which suggest the fearful aspects of things seen in the twilight.

Zwielicht.

Nº 10.
Langsam.
6
Dämm'rung will die Flü_gel sprei_ten, schau_rig rüh_ren
11
ritard.
sich die Bäu_me, Wol_ken zieh'n wie schwe_re Träu_me, was will die_ses Grau'n be_
15
Im Tempo.
deu_ten? Hast ein Reh du lieb vor an_dern, lass es nicht al_lei_ne gra_sen,

20
ritard.
Jä - ger zieh'n im Wald und bla - sen, Stimmen hin und wie - der wan - dern.
ritard.
p
pp
24
Im Tempo.
Hast du ei - nen Freund hie - nie - den, trau' ihm nicht zu die - ser Stun - de.
Im Tempo.
28
freund - lich wohl mit Aug' und Mun - de, sinnt er Krieg im tück' - schen Frie - den.
32
Was heut' ge - het mü - de un - ter, hebt sich mor - gen neu ge - bo - ren.
37
Manches geht in Nacht ver - lo - ren, hü - te dich, sei wach und mun - ter!
R.S.137.

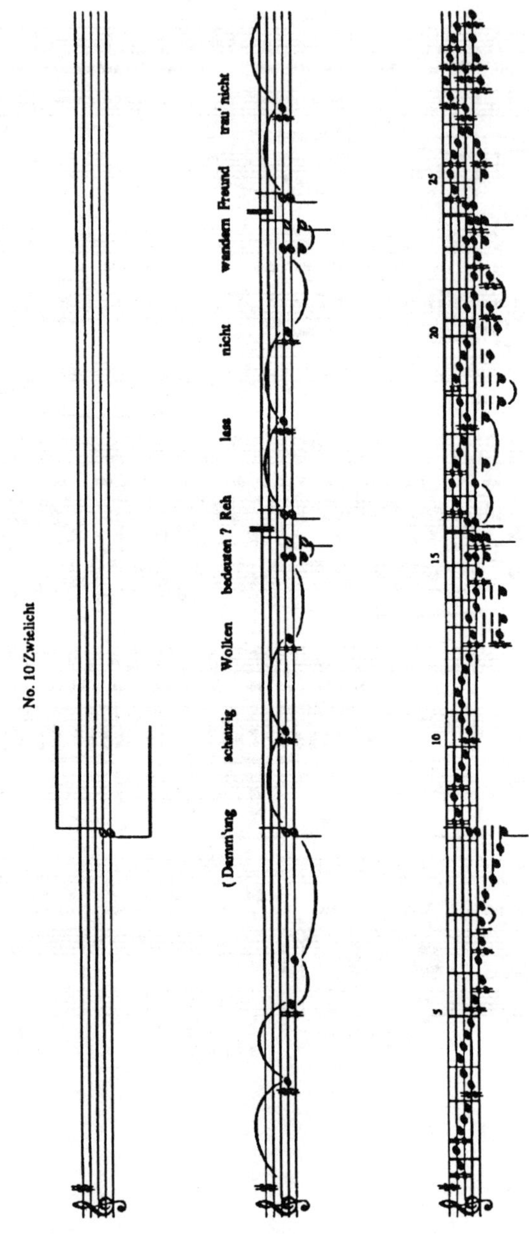
No. 10 Zwielicht
(Damm'ung schaurig Wolken bedeuten ? Reh lass nicht wandern Freund trau' nicht
5
10
15
20
25

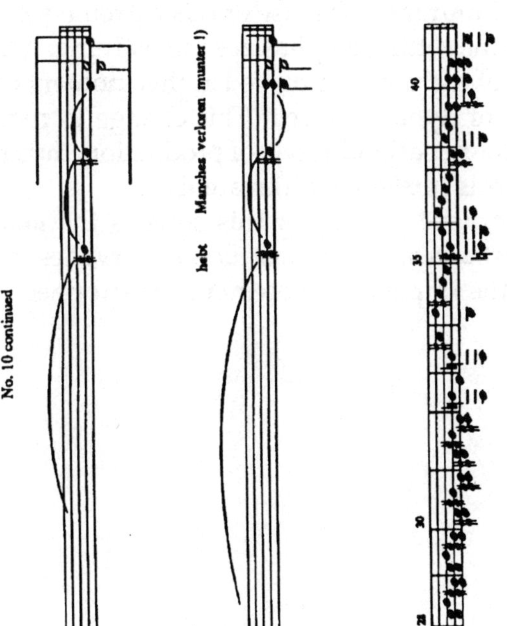
No. 10 continued
hebt Manches verloren munter !)

Schumann's setting of "Zwielicht" is every bit as ambiguous and disturbing in its harmonic content and relations as Eichendorff's poem is in its images and tone of voice. Schumann achieves this through the frequent use of diminished seventh chords and a rhythmically ambiguous piano accompaniment.

The setting of the first two strophes uses the diminished seventh harmonic construction to accompany most of the text and does not make a strong statement of E minor until meas. 23. The third strophe begins like the first two but then explodes with a sequential passage based on the diminished harmony mentioned above (meas. 27-31). The setting of the fourth strophe begins with an extended passage of secondary function which is accompanied by a static rhythmic figure in the right hand of the piano. This radical change in texture serves to differentiate the proverb-like statement of the fourth strophe from the first three strophes which are more illustrative in nature.

The first statement of tonic in the fourth strophe comes at the mention of what may be lost in the night. It is followed by an augmented sixth chord which accompanies the warning "hüte dich, sei wach und munter!" The use of this extremely colorful chord at this point in the setting emphasizes the warning. Furthermore, the low register of the voice employed at this moment causes a natural diminishing of dynamic level. This change in register forces the voice into a more parlando style of production, thus the character of the vocal part is hushed and threatening.

The crucial gesture of this song is the *diminished seventh harmonic construction*. This construction pervades the setting and is used to set the imperative statements of strophes two, three, and four.

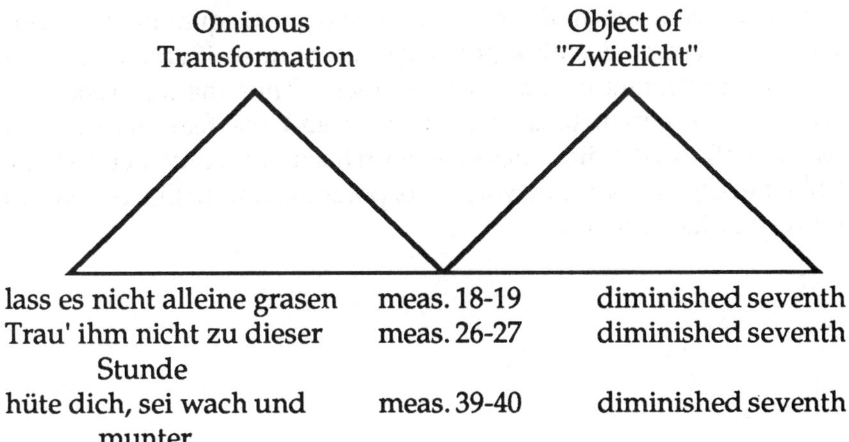

The ground of the intersemiotic relation between Eichendorff's "Zwielicht" and Schumann's setting is *ambiguity*. This quality is best exemplified in the image of the hunting horns whose sound is beautiful but which also stands for imminent danger and the need to beware. Likewise, the diminished seventh harmonic construction is a highly ambiguous musical sign. It is made up of three identical intervals which are not necessarily identified with any one tonality. Furthermore, this harmonic construction can modulate in such a way that it sounds illogical to the listener.

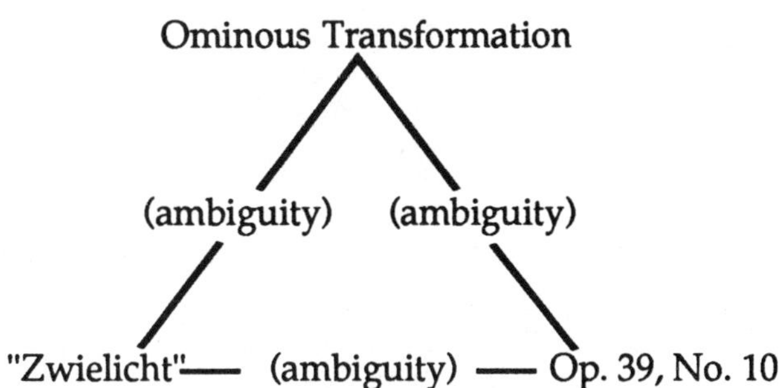

Yet how can the diminished seventh harmonic construction stand for ominous transformation in this setting and secrecy in Op. 39, No. 4? The answer is that, in and of itself, the diminished seventh construction means nothing, it is a mere acoustic quality; however, when it is coupled with a poetic representamen it can stand as a lyrical interpretant of that representmen. Thus the difference between the inherent tension in secrecy and the fear involved in twilight allows the diminished seventh harmonic construction to be linked to Op. 39. No. 4 by way of its potential and to Op. 39, No. 10 by way of its ambiguity.

Eichendorff's "Im Walde" comes from the *Wanderlieder* section of his collected works. It continues to examine the ominous aspects of nature already encountered in the previous four poems. This poem also represents a mid-point in the temporal progression from twilight to darkness which is begun in "Zwielicht" and completed in "Frühlingsnacht." Schumann changes "schauert" to "schauert's" in the final line of the poem.

XI. Prosodic

IM WALDE

Es zog eine Hochzeit den Berg entlang,
Ich hörte die Vögel schlagen,
Da blitzen viel Reiter, das Waldhorn klang,
Das war ein lustiges Jagen!

Und eh' ich's gedacht, war alles verhallt,
Die Nacht bedecket die Runde,
Nur von den Bergen noch rauschet der Wald
Und mich schauert im Herzensgrunde.

XI. Accentual

IM WALDE

zog Hochzeit Berg entlang
hörte Vögel schlagen
blitzen Reiter Waldhorn klang
war lustiges Jagen

eh' gedacht alles verhallt
Nacht bedecket Runde
nur (von) Bergen rauschet Wald
schauert Herzensgrunde

XI. Semantic

IM WALDE

Hochzeit entlang--Vögel schlagen--blitzen Reiter--Waldhorn klang

eh' gedacht alles verhallt

Nacht bedecket--rauschet Wald--schauert Herzensgrunde

XI. Mimetic

IM WALDE

entlang		gedacht
schalgen		verhallt
	vs.	
blitzen		rauschet
klang		schauert

XI. Soliloquizing

IM WALDE

Wald rauschet--schauert Herzensgrunde

Eichendorff's "Im Walde" exhibits many close connections to other poems in this cycle. Because of its placement following "Wehmut" and "Zwielicht," it creates ominous expectations for the reader as the fearful aspects of nightfall are examined. Furthermore, it gains an extended and intensified significance from its use of images crucial to other poems in the cycle.

The ominous interpretants of the central images from the first strophe are all supplied by the memory of the reader from elsewhere in the cycle. The situation can be diagrammed as follows:

Fear

"Hochzeit"	"Braut weinet" No. 7 (isolation)
"Vögel schalgen"	"einsam singen" No. 7 (isolation)
"Waldhornklang"	"Jäger blasen" No.10 (ominous transformation)
	"Waldhorn her und hin" No.3 (irrational attraction)
"Nacht bedecket"	"Zwielicht" No. 10 (ominous transformation)
"Reiter"	"reitst du einsam" No.3 (irrational attraction)

The sign involving the wedding requires some explanation. The image of a wedding was an extremely suggestive event in which to place the object of isolation in "Auf einer Burg," and the theme of isolation certainly is present in "Im Walde." Yet, the setting for the wedding is different in the two poems. In "Auf einer Burg" the wedding takes place in the valley, while in "Im Walde" the wedding proceeds along the mountain. In Eichendorff's work the image of the mountain is used as an indexical sign whose height stands for a connection between earth and heaven. Thus the wedding upon the mountain is a doubly significant image in which an act symbolizing union takes place on a sign of union.

In the last two lines of the poem we are told that only the woods on the mountain continue to rustle after nightfall. This activity is an ominous sign in "Im Walde" because it carries the movement of the past day described in the first strophe into the present of the otherwise silent and inactive night. The other remarkable aspect of the last two lines of this poem is their enjambment. This metrical device serves to temporally relate the two lines in which the acoustically related terms "rauschet" and "schauert" are stated. The fact that every other line in the poem is end-stopped makes the enjambment of the final two lines all the more significant and suggests a certain inexorable relation between their content.

The object of this poem is fear. The signs with which fear is represented involve a progression from activity, seen in the adverbs and verbs of the first strophe, to inactivity, seen in the verbs of the second strophe. The opposition between active and inactive terms is not only a semantic one, it also involves acoustical qualities. The active terms of the first strophe are related by *-en* or *-ng* endings, while the inactive terms are related by *-t* endings. Given this opposition between the activities of the day and the inactivity of the night and the enjambment of the final two lines, the acoustic relation between "rauschet" and "schauert" is all the more poignant, suggesting that all that remains of the day's pleasant activities is the ominous rustling of the forest and the shuddering heart of the narrator. The crucial seme of the poem is the *semantic and acoustic opposition* between the terms of the first and second strophes.

Im Walde.
No. 11.
Ziemlich lebendig.
ritard.
Es zog ei_ne Hoch_zeit den Berg ent_lang,
Im Tempo
ich hör_te die Vö_gel
schla_gen;
Im Tempo.
da blitz_ten viel Rei_ter, das
Wald_horn klang,
das war ein lu_sti_ges Ja_gen!

R.S.127.

20
ritard.
Und eh' ich's ge_dacht, war al_les verhallt.
Im
ritard.
pp
26
p
ritard.
Tempo
Die Nacht be_de_cket die
ritard.
31
p
Rau_de,
Im Tempo.
nur von den Ber_gen noch rau_schet der Wald,
37
und mich schau_ert's im Her_zens_grun_de,
43
und mich schau_ert's im Her_zens_grun_de.
pp

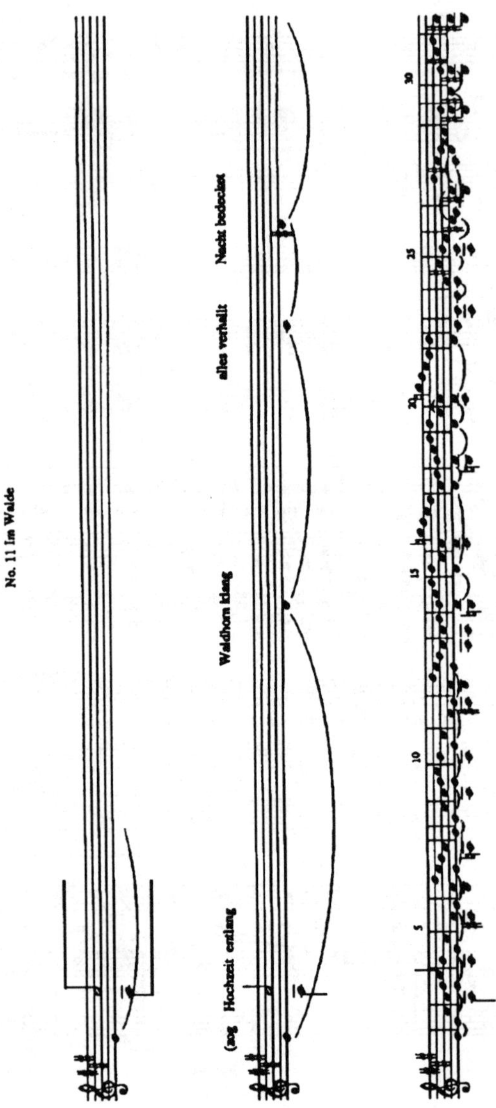
No. 11 Im Walde
(zog Hochzeit entlang
Waldhorn klang
alles verhallt
Nacht bedeckt

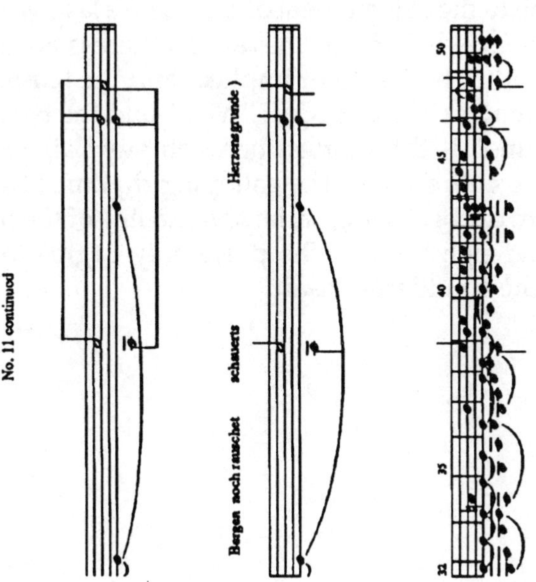
No. 11 continued
Bergen noch rauschet
schauerts
Herzensgrunde)
32
35
40
45
50

Schumann's setting of "Im Walde" focuses upon the connection between the images of the poem to others within the cycle which examine the relations of human beings and nature. The musical means by which Schumann guides the listener toward an understanding of the images in "Im Walde" have to do with tempo and rhythm. The song is marked "Ziemlich lebendig," or "rather lively," yet at the mention of "Hochzeit den Berg entlang," "Vögel schalgen," "war alles verhallt," and "Nacht bedecket die Runde," Schumann instructs the vocalist and pianist to slow the tempo. As will be recalled, both the image of the wedding and the singing bird refer to the theme of isolation in "Auf einer Burg." Thus the slowing of the musical pace of this setting in meas. 3-4 and 9-10 serves to direct the attention of the listener backwards in the cycle. The slowing of the tempo in meas. 24-25 and 30-31 is more of an iconic sign which relates the onset of nightfall with a slowing of activity. The *fluctuation in tempo* indicated by Schumann is the crucial musical gesture of this setting.

Schumann pairs the occasional slowing of tempo with a galloping 6/8 rhythmic figure accompanied by harmonies typically associated with the Waldhorn. This galloping rhythm serves an analogous function to the enjambment of the poem's last two lines. At the point in the song where these lines are set there is not even a hint of ritardando, either indicated or implied, and the temporal distance between the end of the singing of "Wald" and the beginning of the singing of "und" is the shortest between any pair of consecutive phrases in the entire song. The galloping rhythmic figure remains constant from the beginning of the seventh line of the poem into the middle of the eighth line. The pulse only begins to slow at the mention of the shuddering heart.

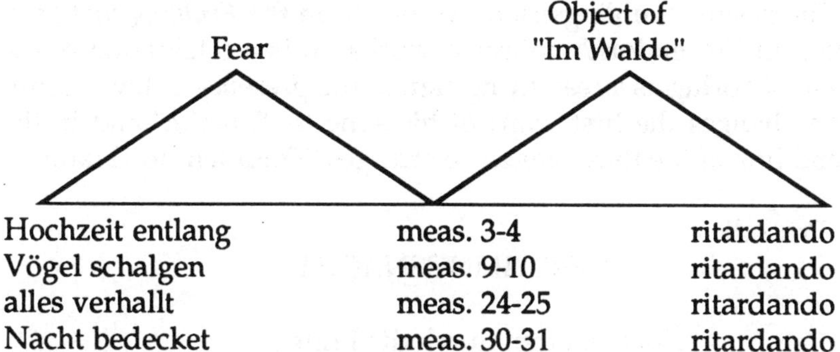

Hochzeit entlang	meas. 3-4	ritardando
Vögel schalgen	meas. 9-10	ritardando
alles verhallt	meas. 24-25	ritardando
Nacht bedecket	meas. 30-31	ritardando

Beginning in meas. 38 and continuing until the end of the setting a slowing of tempo is composed into the vocal line and the accompaniment. All of the note values increase and the 6/8 character of the setting is virtually absent.

The intersemiotic relationship at work in this song involves the opposition between the active terms of the first strophe of the poem and the inactive terms of the second. The lyrical interpretants of these poetic representamens of the onset of nightfall and its attendant fears are the fluctuations in tempo of the setting. The ground of this intersemiotic relationship is *vacillation*. Vacillation is suggested in the poem's progression from activity to inactivity, and it is literally depicted in the narrator's shuddering heart. Vacillation is re-presented in the setting by the numerous fluctuations in tempo.

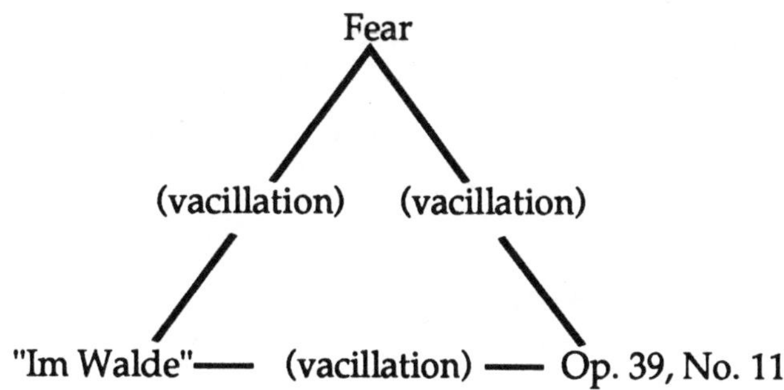

The poem "Frühlingsnacht" comes from the *Frühling und Liebe* section of Eichendorff's collected works. It is a celebration of the arrival of spring as a reassuring sign of the presence of love. Schumann changes the first word of his song to "Über'm" and in the second line of the third stanza he changes "Träumen" to "Traume."

XII. Prosodic

FRÜHLINGSNACHT

Übern Garten durch die Lüfte
Hört ich Wandervögel ziehn,
Das bedeutet Frühlingsdüfte,
Unten fängts schon an zu blühn.

Jauchzen möcht ich, möchte weinen,
Ist mirs doch, als könnts nicht sein,
Alte Wunder wieder scheinen
Mit dem Mondesglanz herein.

Und der Mond, die Sterne sagen's,
Und in Träumen rauscht's der Hain,
Und die Nachtigallen schalgen's:
"Sie ist deine, sie ist dein!"

XII. Accentual

FRÜHLINGSNACHT

übern Garten durch Lüfte
hört Wandervögel ziehn
das bedeutet Frühlingsdüfte
unten fängts an blühn

jauchzen möcht möchte weinen
ist doch könnts (nicht) sein
alte Wunder wieder scheinen
mit Mondesglanz herein

Mond Sterne sagen's
Träumen rauscht's Hain
Nachtigallen schlagen's
sie deine, sie dein

XII. Semantic

FRÜHLINGSNACHT

Wandervögel bedeutet Frühlingsdüfte

jauchzen möcht möchte weinen

Mond, Sterne, Träumen, Hain sagen's:
Nachtigallen schalgen's: sie deine, sie dein

XII. Mimetic

FRÜHLINGSNACHT

weinen		
scheinen	vs.	dein
Hain		

XII. Soliloquizing

FRÜHLINGSNACHT

möcht, möchte
deine, dein

Unlike many of the poems which precede it, Eichendorff's "Frühlingsnacht" represents a celebration, it revels in a world in which images and events have a consistent and positive meaning. For this reason the object of the poem is epiphany, or the grasping of a transcendent reality in a moment of insight into an actual state of affairs. The poem immediately places the reader upon familiar ground, in the midst of nature and in the presence of birds. Eichendorff offers a positive interpretation of this world in the line "Das bedeutet Frühlingsdüfte." Thus he tells us that the poem's title has no ominous overtones and that the signs of spring, migrating birds and budding flowers, do indeed mean spring is coming.

The second stanza presents the emotional response to this unified situation. The narrator tells us both rejoicing and crying are possible. Yet the tears of the narrator of "Frühlingsnacht" are not related to those of the bride in "Auf einer Burg;" rather, they are a corrective for those earlier tears. The following lines reaffirm this corrective function when they refer to the moon's glowing and the stars' speech. These images recall the metaphorical union of heaven and earth as lovers in "Mondnacht." The epiphanic content of the poem is most easily seen in the image of the "alten Wunder." Miracles are traditionally signs of spiritual awakening and insight, and the "old wonders" of this poem seem to be the eternally recurring signs of spring recounted in the first strophe. Thus the epiphany is concerned with the beauty and significance of nature, and it is represented by a renewed appreciation of the signs of spring.

The third strophe involves an accumulation of signs conveying the specific nature of epiphany; the fact that the narrator and the beloved are united. All of these signs stand for the epiphanic moment and simultaneously refer back to other instances of their use in previous poems. Some of them reinforce positive meanings, and others correct negative connotations.

Epiphany

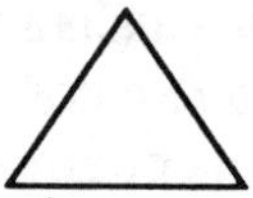

△

Mond sagen's (reinforces union No. 5)	sie ist dein
Sterne sagen's (reinforces union No. 5)	sie ist dein
Hain rauscht's (reinforces union No. 5) (corrects fear No. 11)	sie ist dein
Nachtigallen schlagen's (reinforces union No. 5) (corrects isolation No. 7)	sie ist dein

The most striking characteristics of this poem are its almost literal repetition of many terms and its excited accumulation of signs of epiphany. It is this *repetitive and emotionally charged tone* which is the seme of the poem.

Frühlingsnacht.
Nº 12.
Ziemlich rasch. Leidenschaftlich.
p
Ue - berm Gar - - ten durch die
3
Lüf - te hört' ich Wan - der - vö - gel zieh'n; das be -
6
deu - tet Früh - - lings - düf - te, un - ten fängt's schon an zu
ritard.
9
Im Tempo.
blüh'n. Jauch - zen möcht' ich, möchte wei - nen, ist mir's
12
doch, als könnt's nicht sein! Al - le Wun - der wie - - der
R.S.127.

15
ritard.
schei - nen mit dem Mon - desglanz her - ein.
ritard.
Im Tempo
18
Und der Mond, die Ster - ne sa - gen's, und im
21
Trau - me rauscht's der Hain, und die Nach - ti - gal - len
24
schla - gen's: „Sie ist Dei - ne, sie ist Dein!“
27
ritard.

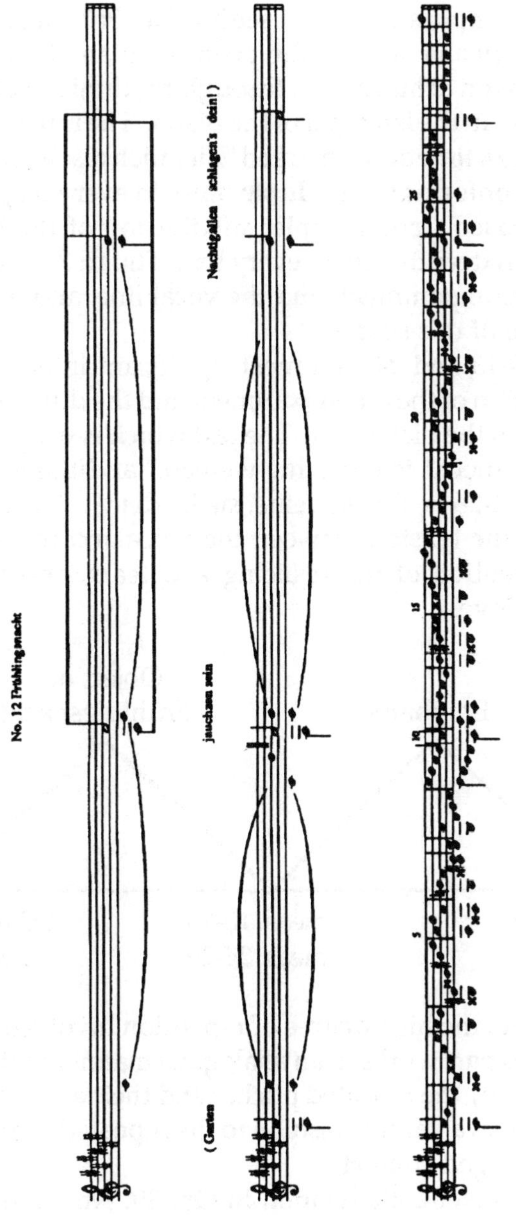
No. 12 Frühlingsnacht
(Garten
jauchzen sein
Nachtigallen schlagen's drein!)

Schumann supplies a musical setting for "Frühlingsnacht" that matches the epiphanic tone of the poem with an effusive musical energy. Schumann achieves this through rhythmic relations and a repeated gesture in the left hand of the piano. The musical setting of this poem is in 2/4 time and is marked "Ziemlich rasch" or rather fast. The vocal line conforms to this duple pulse in every respect, yet the piano part is based upon a triplet subdivision of the beat and is displaced by a sixteenth note in every bar. Thus a *3:2 relation* exists between the accompaniment and the vocal line, and is the crucial musical gesture of this setting.

In meas. 10-13 and 24-29 a most significant integration of the triplet subdivision of the accompaniment and the duple pulse of the melody occurs in the piano part. The text which is sung in meas. 10-13 is "jauchzen möcht ich, möchte weinen," and the text which is sung in meas. 24-26 is "Sie ist deine, sie ist dein!" Thus Schumann makes explicit the tension between the voice and the accompaniment at the mention of the rejoicing and tears, and the ecstatic reassurance of love.

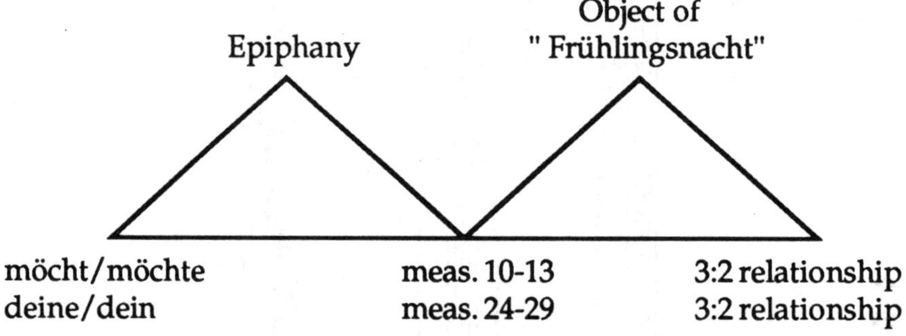

Furthermore, the high degree of repetition involved in the bass line of the piano part works in an analogous manner to the repeated terms in the poem; the repeated pitches and their ascending motion generate energy in a parallel fashion to the repeated terms and their emotionally charged context.

Thus the intersemiotic relation in Op. 39, No. 12 involves the repeated terms "möcht/möchte" and "deine/dein" which serve as signs of epiphany, while the musical setting makes use of a 3:2 relationship between its piano and vocal parts. The ground of this relationship is *profusion*. Profusion is involved in epiphany inasmuch as the epiphanic moment is one in which a complex of signs work to communicate truth. Profusion is seen in the poem in the numerous voices which speak, rustle, and sing the unity of the two lovers. Profusion is re-presented in the setting by the extremely repetitive accompaniment figures and the repeated bass line.

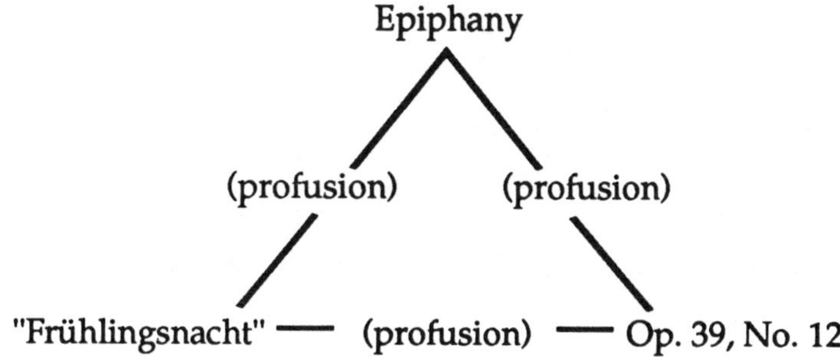

CONCLUSION

In the brief introduction to the poems of Schumann's Eichendorff cycle in his *Ring of Words* Philip Miller states, "Schumann's cycle is made up of twelve selected Eichendorff poems. Indeed, there is little connection between them. But as a series of brief mood pictures, they make a satisfying group, they are often sung together" (1973, 34). While a cursory reading or hearing may seem to support this statement, the previous analysis shows a remarkably consistent poetic tone which is amply reinforced by the harmonic design of Schumann's settings.

As the first poem suggests and as the last poem confirms, this cycle examines the evolving significance of a uniform set of images in the context of a dream state. This dream state, which is reinforced by the nocturnal settings and the mention of dreams in many of the poems, serves as a general metaphor, or poetic tonality, for the entire cycle. The most ubiquitous of the images used in the cycle are the singing bird, the rustling forest, and the ringing Waldhorn. All of these images are given both negative and positive connotations as they are experienced in the dream state of the cycle. The bird's song which is present in Op. 39, Nos. 2, 4, 7, 8, 9, and 11 is both doleful and beautiful. The forest's rustling which is present in Op. 39, Nos. 6, 7, 8, 11, and 12 is both ominous and reassuring. And the horn's ringing, present in Op. 39, Nos. 3, 10, and 11, signifies both danger and excitement. Generally speaking, the evolution of the significance of these images progresses from negative to positive.

The general harmonic context in which this cycle functions involves a progression from the F# minor tonality of the first setting to the F# major tonality of the last setting. The tonality of five of the intervening settings focuses upon either E major or E minor (Op. 39, Nos. 3, 5, 7, 9, and 10). These settings deal mostly with the ominous connotations of images encountered in the dream state. The only exception to these negative connotations is Op. 39, No. 5 which examines the longing for union with nature. Op. 39, Nos. 2, 4, 6, 8, and 11 are in varied tonalities and, for the most part, examine the positive connotations of the images encountered in the dream state. The two exceptions to this generalization are Op. 39, No. 8 and Op. 39, No.11. Op. 39, No.8 has confusion as its object; however, this song is connected harmonically to Op. 39, No. 7 which is in the key of E minor.

The gestural-semiotic approach to Schumann's Eichendorff poetry in his Liederkries Op. 39 also yields important information in regard to Eichendorff criticism, Schumann interpretation, and a critical approach to nineteenth- century Lieder.

The most significant result of this study pertaining to Eichendorff's poetry, its interpretation and estimation, comes in regard to its gestural qualities. Rather than viewing his work as popular lyrics of nature, or even a naive metaphysics, the qualities of repetition, unity, and ambiguity should be understood as musical analogues. His use of a limited lexicon of natural images and the way these images contribute to an extremely uniform structure resemble musical organization. Such an approach to these aspects of Eichendorff's work offers a new direction for Eichendorff scholarship.

The implications of this study in regard to Schumann, and Schumann scholarship, have to do with his conception of music as simultaneously expressive and reflexive. This direction is suggested by Schumann's own writings in which the function of music is referred to as *Auflösung*. Schumann's conception of song as *nachwirken* implies that song is a re-presentation of a poem, at once determined by the poem but not limited in its own significance by that determination.

The gestural-semiotic theory of Lied composition employed in this study identifies and defines an intersemiotic quality, present in both poem and setting, which serves as the vehicle for intersemiotic transmutation. Admittedly, the analysis which this theory enables does not account for either the poem or its musical setting in their entirety. However, it does demonstrate that the semiosis of Lieder is a process of intersemiotic transmutation in which a poetic representamen determines a melopoetic interpretant which can then function as a representamen capable of determining its own triadic relationship, or more simply put, the manner in which Schumann's setting re-presents Eichendorff's magic word.

To be sure, Schumann's Eichendorff Lieder and the nineteenth-century approach to song represent an exceptional conflation of language and music, of poetic seme and musical gesture. Yet the relation between poem and song explicated by Peirce's semiotic and Mead's theory of gesture as employed in this study can be projected into other instances of song in which the correspondence between poem and setting is not so eloquent.

APPENDIX ONE: ON SEMIOTIC

Aside from ascribing the overt origins of semiotic to Saussure and Peirce, there seems to be a drive to place the implicit origins of the theory of signs as far into the past as possible, as if this will lend further support to the rather universal claims of application made by this way of thinking. Two of the most popular and well-considered placements of the origins of semiotic have been offered by John Deely in his *Introducing Semiotic* and Terrence Hawkes in his *Structuralism and Semiotics*. Deely wishes to trace the origins of semiotic in the work of John of St. Thomas and Hawkes in the work of Giambattista Vico.

John of St. Thomas (1589-1644) was Spanish, a member of the clergy, and thoroughly scholastic in his philosophical orientation. His first mention of signs and their role in signification comes in his *Material Logic*. In the chapter titled "On Signs, Cognitions, and Concepts," John of St. Thomas defined a sign as "that which represents something other than itself to a cognitive power" (1955, 380). In this same chapter he distinguished between conventional signs and natural signs. Conventional signs are those which have significance and convey meaning because we, as human beings, ascribe meaning to them. An obvious example of a conventional sign is a word upon the page of a book. John of St. Thomas conceived of natural signs as elements of nature or related to nature through which God's existence was made known to human kind (1955, 390-91).

John of St. Thomas valued natural signs far more than conventional signs. In a later work, *Tractatus de Signis*, which has been handsomely translated and annotated by Deely, John of St. Thomas investigated at length the nature of these natural signs and erected a typology of divine signification within the constructs of Aristotelian logic.

Giambattista Vico (1668-1744) was Italian, a very progressive thinker for his day, and an extremely original social theorist. In his *New Science* Vico undertook a rather idiosyncratic account of Western social history as well as a philosophical assessment of that history. Vico was interested in the manner in which human beings go about "making" their world and in their continual creation of recognizable and repeated forms. In this regard Vico stated:

> The nature of institutions is nothing but their coming into being at certain times and in certain guises. Whenever the time and guise are thus and so, such and not otherwise are the institutions that come into being (1970, 147).

Thus it is obvious that Vico's thought should be important to the structuralist, but his mention of signs and signification does not constitute a semiotic theory. Rather, Vico was concerned with the manner in which language arose and led to further developments in civilization. His mention of signs was scant and always made in relation to the continuum of social development.

This is not to suggest that the work of Deely and Hawkes in regard to the placement of the implicit origins of semiotic in the thought of John of St. Thomas and of Vico is to be discounted. Quite the contrary, it is extremely important to see the role that signs and thinking about signs played in western thought. There is, however, a thinker whose work had immeasurable impact upon semiotic and semiotic thinking who is yet to be discussed in this regard. He is far better known than either John of St. Thomas or Vico, his work is vastly more influential than theirs', and he was almost certainly known to Saussure and Peirce.

Immanuel Kant

In his *Critique of Pure Reason*, a work which may well signal the advent of modernity, Immanuel Kant (1724-1804) proposed to investigate the limits of human reason. Kant forsook the search for knowledge of things in themselves and instead turned his attention to the way in which things are known to a subject. He stated in the preface to the second edition of his first critique:

> The attempt to alter the procedure which has hitherto prevailed in metaphysics, by completely revolutionising it in accordance with the example set by the geometers and the physicists, forms indeed the main purpose of this critique of pure speculative reason. It is a treatise on the method, not a system of the science itself (Kant 1965, Bxxii).

In a footnote to this passage, Kant further defined the type of revolution which he was undertaking by recalling the work of Copernicus who "dared in a manner contradictory to the senses, but yet true, to seek the observed movements, not in the heavenly bodies, but in the spectator." Kant used the term revolution in a most literal sense; of turning from one mode of thinking about objects to another mode of thinking about the intuiting subject. The revolution he posited and then explicated in his first critique is, in fact, still with us today.

There are two critical aspects of the revolution Kant promises present in the passages above and throughout his whole project which cannot be overemphasized. The first is that his work is methodological in substance: it is about a way of looking at things, and not about the things themselves. Secondly, it promises no knowledge of things—no increase in the understanding of our world—only an evaluation of ourselves as intuiting subjects. This methodological and subjective focus typifies thinking and scholarship since Kant and has contributed in a direct, though unexplored, manner to semiotic thought and practice. For semiotic is a method which claims to be universal in its application and treats all things as the extension of subjective consciousness—as signs.

Kant's essential contention in the *Critique of Pure Reason* is that we have no access to things in themselves, to objects; rather we know them only as appearances in space and time. In the section of his first critique titled "Transcendental Aesthetic," Kant dealt with space and time as pure forms of intuition, as ways of perceiving things which the subject brings to its relation with the object, and which are all that the subject will ever be afforded in the way of knowledge of the object. Hence the only recourse to the object available to the subject is through the pure intuitions of space and time. Kant stated:

> By means of outer sense, a property of mind, we represent toourselves objects as outside us, and all without exception in space...Inner sense, by means of which the mind intuits itself or its innerstate, yields indeed no intuition of the soul itself as an object; but there is nevertheless a determinate form (namely time) in which alone the intuition of inner states is possible...What then are space and time? Are they real existences? Are they only determinations or relations of things, yet such as would belong to things even if they were not intuited? Or are space and time such that they belong only to the form of intuition, and therefore to the subjective constitution of our mind, apart from which they could not be ascribed to anything whatsoever (1965, B37-38).

It is the last of these three alternatives which Kant accepted as the true nature of the pure forms of intuition, space and time.

Kant referred to the manner in which objects appeared to the pure forms of intuition as a "manifold." The manifold has the quality of being at once accessible to the pure intuition of space by which it is grasped all at once, and accessible to the pure intuition of time which grasps the manifold in a discursive manner, as a succession of many folds layered one on top of the other in accordion-like fashion. Thus, for Kant, space and time are pure forms of intuition which exist between perception and abstraction, they are *a priori* elements of human understanding.

Kant did not, however, view space and time as equal in nature. His description of the character of each can be outlined in the following manner:

SPACE	TIME
- we can never represent to ourselves the absence of space	- we can never remove time from appearances
- yet we can think of space as empty of objects	- but we can remove appearances from time
- thus space is the condition of the possibility of appearances	- thus time is given *a priori,* appearances may vanish, but time cannot be removed

Thus time has a privileged status. Space makes appearances or outer sensations possible, but time makes possible the human intuition needed to perceive those appearances. Time is given *a priori* as that which is presupposed in both inner and outer sense.

These realizations about space and time lead Kant to four important conclusions about human intuition and its relation to objects:

(1) The things we intuit are not, in themselves, what we intuit them as being. They are representations of appearance (1965, A42/B59).

(2) We know ourselves as we appear to ourselves, not as we are (1965, B67).

(3) It is only if we ascribe objective reality to our forms of intuition that everything we know becomes illusion (1965, B69).

(4) Our mode of intuition is dependent upon the existence of an object and is possible only if the intuitive subject is affected by the object (1965, B71n).

The way in which Kant's *Critique of Pure Reason* is related to semiotic thinking and criticism has to do with the manifold and the the sign. Kant's manifold pertains to the way in which the reality of the object is perceived by the subject. Likewise, the notion of sign pertains to the way in which the object signified is made known to the subject. Furthermore, the manifold is known in space and time, it can be grasped both all at once and successively. Following Saussure's basic observation, the sign is grasped connotatively as a configuration of meaning and denotatively as a part of a succession of meaning.

APPENDIX TWO: ON GESTURE

The concept of gesture is typically used to describe an early stage of, or accompaniment to, linguistic communication. George Herbert Mead is the most important thinker to deal with gesture in this sense, but the context in which he discusses gesture is one with a strictly linguistic bias. There is another tradition of looking at gesture, however, which is not as well known but nevertheless important to this study. This other approach sees gesture in a more autonomous light as the original form of human expression, linguistic or otherwise, as well as the original element of social interaction.

Giambattista Vico

As will be recalled from the discussion of his *New Science* in relation to semiotic, Vico's work is a speculative history of social development. In it, Vico divided history into three eras or stages. The first is the age of the Gods, which is typified by gestural expression and commanded by oracles. The second is the age of heroes, which is typified by poetic expression and commanded by the heroes themselves. And the third is the age of men, which is typified by prose or legal-ese and ruled by a popular commonwealth (Vico 1970, 3). Vico founded his speculative pseudo-history on the truth he found inherent in poetic creation. In the section of his *New Science* titled "Corollaries Concerning the Origins of Languages and Letters; and, Therein, the Origins of Hieroglyphics, Laws, Names, Family Arms, Medals, Money; and Hence of the First Language and Literature of the Natural Law of the Gentes," Vico posited the following principles of the origin of language:

(1) That the first men conceived ideas of things by imaginative characters of animate and mute substances.

(2) That they expressed themselves by means of gestures or physical objects which had natural relations with the ideas; for example three ears of grain, or acting as if swinging a scythe three times, to signify three years.

(3) That they expressed themselves by a language with natural significations (1970, 98).

As an example of these principles, Vico posited a myth of the primordial act of naming, the origin of language—the naming of Jove. The scenario involves primitive individuals faced with a fierce thunderstorm which provokes in them great fear. In an effort to assimilate, and thus diminish, the frightful elements of the storm the individuals quake along with the thunder and lightning. In a final effort to internalize the storm they name *both* the internal quaking and the external storm "Jove." Vico stated, "whatever these men saw, imagined, or even made or did themselves they believed to be Jove; and all the universe which came within their scope, and all its parts, they gave the being of animate substance" (1970, 76-77).

The mythical equation of objects with gestures—of thunder with bodily quaking—constitutes what Vico calls a hieroglyphic language. In short it is a language in which things are words and words are things. This concept is the central principle of Vico's philosophy and he calls it *verum-factum*. The principle of *verum-factum* is at the heart of Vico's theorizing about the origin of language in which the matter of truth has, until recent years, been assumed and the matter of making has remained clouded. Furthermore, it is extremely important for the question of the origin of aesthetic expression, in which the matter of creation is overt and the matter of truth more often suspect.

In discussing the manner in which this hieroglyphic language, based upon the principle of *verum-factum*, evolves into a spoken and eventually written language, Vico made the following distinctions which shed further light on the discussion of song, and its poetic and musical components.

> The language of the Gods was almost entirely mute, only very slightly articulate; the language of the heroes, an equal mixture of articulate and mute;...the language of men, almost entirely articulate and only very slightly mute... Thus necessarily the heroic language was in the beginning disordered to the extreme; and this is a great source of the obscurity of fables (1970, 106).

The most obvious application of this myth of the origin of various forms of expression to the phenomenon of song is in relation to poetry. Perhaps the most distinctive aspect of poetry is the manner in which it can manipulate logical or discursive word order for aesthetic affect. This is the meaning of the rhetorical device of hyperbaton. Thus the age of the heroes, typified by poetry or fable, is an age which uses language in an expressive rather than rational manner. Moreover, the language which Vico attributed to the age of the Gods, which is only very slightly articulate, is analogous to music. This assertion rests on the opinion that Vico's use of "articulate" in this context alludes to the manner in which the language was physically produced as opposed to a more structural or abstract use of the term. This reading is supported by the manner in which Vico opposes "articulate" with "mute" in this passage.

In relation to muteness Vico states, "Mutes utter formless sounds by singing, and stammerers by singing teach their tongues to pronounce" (1970, 35). Vico places song as a form of expression alongside poetry in the age of the heroes and speculates at length about the manner in which Homer's epics might have been sung. However, the passages alluded to above are sufficient to suggest that the age of the Gods was one in which human expression took on musical characteristics; non-verbal, evocative, audible movement in time.

Ernst Cassirer

In the first volume of his *Philosophy of Symbolic Forms* Ernst Cassirer (1874-1945) outlined a morphology of human expression, employing a system designed to address the cultural sciences (1953, 69). He inquired into the origin of human expression and posited gestural movement as the fundamental factor in the structure of consciousness. He stated that movement is an immediate unity of "inward" and "outward" (1953, 179). He went on to argue that the origin of both reflection and language is in the continuous transition from physical to conceptual grasping (1953, 181).

Cassirer defined physical grasping as a movement which holds or brings a thing into one's presence. Conceptual grasping involves the transition from imitative to indicative gestures (1953, 182). Imitative gestures are the mere mimicry of outward impressions, while indicative gestures are not simply the repetition but the projection of salient characteristics of experience—not merely the reproduction but the representation of selected aspects of a thing.

WORKS CITED

Adorno, Theodor. 1958. Zum Gedaechtnis Eichendorffs. *Noten zur Literatur*. Frankfort am Main: Suhrkamp.

Boetticher, Wolfgang. 1941. *Robert Schumann: Einfuehrung in Persoenalichkeit und Werk*. Berlin: Hahnfeld.

Buchler, Justus. 1955. *Philosophical Writings of Peirce*. New York: Dover.

Cassirer, Ernst. 1953. *Philosophy of Symbolic Forms*. trans. Manheim, New Haven: Yale University Press.

Coker, Wilson. 1972. *Music and Meaning*. New York: Free Press.

Cone, Edward. 1956. Words into Music. *Sound and Poetry*. ed. Frye, New York: Columbia University Press.

Eichendorff, Joseph von. 1864. *Saemmtliche Werke*. ed. Hermann von Eichendorff, Leipzig: Voigt and Guenther.

Fischer-Dieskau, Dietrich. 1988. *Robert Schumann: Words and Music*. trans. Pauly, Portland: Amadeus Press.

Frye, Northrop. 1957. Melos and Lexis. *Sound and Poetry*. ed. Frye, New York: Columbia University Press.

Jakobson, Roman. 1971(1959). On Linguistic Aspects of Translation. *Selected Writings* II. Paris: Mouton de Gruyter.

John of St. Thomas. 1955. *Material Logic*. trans. Glanville, Hollenhorst, and Simon, Chicago: University of Chicago Press.

Kant, Immanuel. 1965. *Critique of Pure Reason*. trans. Norman Kemp Smith, New York: St. Martin's Press.

Kramer, Lawrence. 1984. *Music and Poetry in the Nineteenth Century and After*. Los Angeles: University of California Press.

Langer, Susanne. 1953. *Feeling and Form*. New York: Scribners

Mead, George Herbert. 1934. *Mind, Self, and Society*. Chicago: University of Chicago Press.

Miller, Philip. 1973. *The Ring of Words*. New York: Norton.

Peirce, Charles Sanders. 1955. *Philosophical Writings of Peirce*. ed. Buchler, New York: Dover.

___________________. 1931-1958. *Collected Papers* I-IV. ed. Hartshorne and Weiss, Cambridge: Harvard University Press.

___________________. 1982- . *Writings of C.S. Peirce* I- , ed. Fisch, Bloomington: Indiana University Press.

Radner, Lawrence. 1970. *Eichendorff: The Spiritual Geometer*. Lafayette: Purdue University Studies.

Schenker, Heinrich. 1935. *Der Freie Satz*. Vienna.

Scher, Steven Paul. 1986. Comparing Poetry and Music: Beethoven's Goethe-Lieder. *Sensus Communis*. ed. Riesz et al, Tuebingen: G Narr.

Schumann, Robert. 1854. *Gesammelte Schriften*. Liepzig: Wigand.

_______________. Die Tonwelt. Unpublished manuscript quoted in Boetticher, *Robert Schumann*. Berlin: Hahnfeld, 1941.

Sebeok, Thomas. 1978. *S ight, Sound, and Sense.* Bloomington: Indiana University Press.

Seidlin, Oscar. 1961. Eichendorff's Symbolic Landscape. *University of North Carolina Studies in Comparative Literature* 30(Spring)141-160.

Silverman, Kaja. 1983. *The Subject of Semiotics.* New York: Oxford University Press.

Thum, Reinhard. 1983. Cliche and Stereotype. *Philological Quarterly* 62 (Summer) 435-457.

Vico, Giambattista. 1970. *The New Science of Giambattista Vico.* trans. Bergin and Fisch, Ithaca: Cornell University Press.

SELECTED BIBLIOGRAPHY

I.General Materials

a.Text-Music Relationships

Barricelli and Gibaldi, eds. 1982. *The Interrelations of Literature*. New York: Modern Langauge Association.

Barzun, Jacques. 1985. *Critical Questions*. Chicago: University of Chicago Press.

Brown, Calvin. 1948. *Music and Literature*. Athens, GA: University of Georgia Press.

____________. 1953. *Tones into Words*. Athens, GA: University of Georgia Press.

Cone, Edward. 1956. Words into Music. *Sound and Poetry*, ed. Frye, New York: Columbia University Press.

Frye, Northrop. 1956. Melos and Lexis. *Sound and Poetry* ed. Frye, New York: Columbia University Press.

Jorgens, Elise. 1982. *The Well-Tun'd Word*. Minneapolis: University of Minnesota Press.

Kramer, Lawrence. 1984. *Music and Poetry in the Nineteenth Century and After*. Los Angeles: University of California Press.

Noske, Frits. 1977. *Signifier and Signified*. Hague: Martinus Nijhoff.

Petri, Horst. 1964. *Literatur und Musik.* Goettingen: Vandenhoek and Ruprecht.

Scher, Steven Paul. 1968. *Verbal Music in German Literature.* New Haven: Yale University Press.

_______________. 1970. Notes Towards a Theory of Verbal Music. *Comparative Literature* 22 (Winter) 147-156.

_______________. 1985. *Literatur und Musik.* Berlin: Erich Schmidt Verlag.

_______________. 1986, Comparing Poetry and Music: Beethoven's Goethe-Lieder. *Sensus Communis.* eds. Riesz et al, Tuebingen: G. Narr.

Siegel, L. 1983. *Music in German Romantic Literature.* Novato: El Ra Publications.

Steiner, Wendy. 1984. *The Sign in Music and Literature.* Austin:University of Texas Press.

Winn, James. 1981. *Unsuspected Eloquence.* New Haven: Yale University Press.

b. Song

Bie, Oscar. 1926. *Das deutsche Lied.* Berlin: Fischer.

Brody, Elaine and Fowkes, Robert. 1971. *The German Lied and its Poetry.* New York: New York University Press.

Georgiages, Thrasybulos. 1967. *Schubert: Musik und Lyrik.* Goettingen: Vandenhoek and Ruprecht.

Hall, James. 1953. *The Art Song*. Norman: University of Oklahoma Press.

Landau, A. 1980. *The Lied*. Arizona: University Press of America.

Mustard, H.M. 1946. *The Lyric Cycle in German Literature*. New York: Norton.

Stein, Jack. 1971. *Poem and Music in the German Lied*. Cambridge: Harvard University Press.

Stevens, Denis. ed. 1970. *A History of Song*. New York: Norton.

Whitton, K. 1984. *Lieder*. London: Julia MacRae.

II.Joseph von Eichendorff

a. Editions

Eichendorff, Joseph von. 1841. *Werke*. Berlin: Simion.

__________. 1864. *Saemmtliche Werke*. ed. Hermann von Eichendorff, Leipzig: Voigt and Guenther.

__________. 1866. *Der deutsche Roman des achtzehnten Jahrhunderts Verhaeltnis zum Christentum*. Paderborn: Schoeningh.

__________. 1866. *Geschichte der poetischen Literature Deutschlands*. Paderborn: Schoeningh.

__________. 1878. *Gedichte*. 8th edition. Leipzig: Guenther.

__________. 1883. *Saemmtliche Poetische Werke*. Liepzig: Amelangs

Verlag.

_________. 1970. *Werke*. ed. Perfahl, Munich: Winkler Verlag.

b. Eichendorff Criticism

Borman, Alexander von. 1968. *Natura Loquitur*. Tuebingen: Niemeyer.

Busse, Eckhard. 1975. *Die Eichendorff-Rezeption im Kunstlied*. Wurzburg.

Haller, Rudolph. 1962. *Eichendorffs Balladenwerk*. Berne: Francke.

Heinisch, Klaus-Joachim. 1966. *Deutsche Romantik*. Paderborn: Schoeningh.

Radner, Lawrence. 1970. *Eichendorff: Spiritual Geometer*. Lafayette: Purdue University Studies.

Seidlin, Oskar. 1961. Eichendorff's Symbolic Landscape. *University of North Carolina Studies in Comparative Literature* 30 (Spring) 141-160.

_________. 1965. *Versuche Ueber Eichendorff*. Goettingen: Vandenhoek and Ruprecht.

Thym, Juergen. 1974. *The Solo Song Settings of Eichendorff's Poetry by Schumann and Wolf*. unpublished dissertation, Ann Arbor: University Microfilms.

III.Robert Schumann

a.Primary Sources

Schumann, Robert. 1888. *Early Letters of Robert Schumann*. trans. Herbert, London: Bell and Sons.

________________. 1871. *Gesammelte Schriften Ueber Musik und Musiker*. Leipzig: Wigand.

________________. 1877. *Music and Musicians*. trans. Ritter, New York: Schuberth.

________________. 1885. *Jugendbriefe von Robert Schumann*. Leipzig: Breitkopf und Haertel.

________________. 1904. *Robert Schumanns Briefe: Neue Folge*. ed. Jensen, Leipzig: Breitkopf und Haertel.

b. Schumann Criticism

Abraham, Gerald, ed. 1952. *Schumann: A Symposium*. London: Oxford University Press.

Boetticher, Wolfgang. 1941. *Robert Schumann*. Berlin: Hahnfeld.

Brion, Marcel. 1956. *Schumann and the Romantic Age*. trans. Sainsbury, London: Collins.

Brown, Thomas. 1968. *The Aesthetics of Robert Schumann*. New York: Philosophical Library.

Chissell, Joan. 1967. *Schumann*. London: Dent.

Desmond, A. 1972. *Schumann Songs*. Seattle: University of Washington Press.

Fischer-Dieskau, Dietrich. 1988. *Robert Schumann: Words and Music*. trans. Pauly, Portland: Amadeus Press.

Knaus, H. 1974. *Musiksprache und Werkstruktur in Robert Schumanns Liederkreis*. Munich.

Lippmann, Edward. 1965. Schumann. *Die Musik in Geschichte und Gegenwart* XII, 272-325.

Plantinga, Leon. 1967. *Schumann as Critic*. New Haven: Yale University Press.

Sams, Eric. 1969. *The Songs of Robert Schumann*. London: Methuen.

Walker, Alan. 1972. *Robert Schumann: The Man and His Music*. London: Barie and Jenkins.

Walsh, S. 1971. *Lieder of Schumann*. New York: Praeger.

IV.Semiotic

a. General Materials

Deely, John. 1982. *Introducing Semiotic*. Bloomington: Indiana University Press.

Eco, Umberto. 1984. *A Theory of Semiotics*. Bloomington: Indiana University Press.

Freeman, E. 1934. *The Categories of Peirce*. London: Open Court.

Guiraud, Pierre. 1975. *Semiology*. trans. Gross, Boston: Routledge and Kegan Paul.

Hawkes, Terrence. 1977. *Structualism and Semiotics*. Los Angeles: University of California Press.

Jakobson, Roman. 1971. *Selected Writings*. Paris: Mouton de Gruyter.

Morris, Charles. 1964. *Signification and Significance*. Cambridge: MIT Press.

____________. 1971. *Writings on the General Theory of Signs*. Hague: Martinus Nijhoff.

Peirce, Charles Sanders. 1953. *Letters to Lady Welby*. ed. Lieb, New Haven: Graduate Philosophy Club.

___________________. 1955. *Philosophical Writings of Peirce*. ed. Buchler, New York: Dover.

___________________. 1931-1958. *Collected Papers* I-IV. ed. Hartshorne and Weiss, Cambridge: Harvard University Press.

___________________. 1982- . *Writings of C. S. Peirce* I- . ed. Fisch, Bloomington: Indiana University Press.

Saussure, Ferdinand. 1959. *Course in General Linguistics*. ed. Bally and Sechehaye, trans. Baskin, New York: McGraw Hill.

Silverman, Kaja. 1983. *The Subject of Semiotics*. New York: Oxford University Press.

b.Semiotic and Music

Coker, Wilson. 1972. *Music and Meaning*. New York: Free Press.

Cole, Hugo. 1974. *Sounds and Signs*. New York: Oxford University Press.

Nattiez, Jean-Jacques. 1975. *Fondements d'une semiologie de la musique.* Paris: Union Generale d'Editions.

Noske, Frits. 1977. *Signifier and Signified.* Hague: Martinus Nijhoff.

Schneider, Reinhard. 1980. *Semiotik der Musik.* Munich: Fink Verlag.

Steiner, Wendy. 1984. *The Sign in Music and Literature.* ed. Steiner, Austin: University of Texas Press.

Tarasti, Eero. 1979. *Myth and Music.* New York: Mouton de Gruyter.

V. Gesture

a. General Materials

Joas, Hans. 1985. *George Herbert Mead: A Contemporary Re-Examination.* Cambridge: MIT Press.

Kang, W. 1976. *George Herbert Mead's Concept of Rationality.* Paris: Mouton de Gruyter.

Mead, George Herbert. 1934. *Mind, Self, and Society.* Chicago: University of Chicago Press.

__________________. 1938. *The Philosophy of the Act.* Chicago: University of Chicago Press.

b. Gesture and Music

Coker, Wilson. 1972. *Music and Meaning.* New York: Free Press.

INDEX

NEW CONNECTIONS:
Studies in Interdisciplinarity

This series has as its focus the interrelationships between literature and the other arts, science, philosophy, law, psychology, anthropology, and religion. Book-length manuscripts of at least 200 pages examining and illustrating the intricacies of these interrelationships will be considered. Comparative studies emphasizing new methods of dealing with critical or theoretical problems between disciplines will be given preference. Consideration will also be given to studies of other humanities disciplines engaged in interdisciplinary dialogues.

The series editor is: Shirley Paolini
Barry University
11300 N.E. 2nd Avenue
Miami Shores, Florida 33161